NEW TESTA

Gene *al E itor*
A.T.

REVELATION

REVELATION

John M. Court

Sheffield Academic Press

In memory of Tingri

First published by JSOT Press 1994
Reprinted 1999

Copyright © 1994, 1999 Sheffield Academic Press

Published by Sheffield Academic Press Ltd
Mansion House
19 Kingfield Road
Sheffield S11 9AS
England

Typeset by Sheffield Academic Press
and
Printed on acid-free paper in Great Britain by
The Cromwell Press
Trowbridge, Wiltshire

British Library Cataloguing in Publication Data

A catalogue record for this book is available
from the British Library

ISBN 1-85075-705-4

CONTENTS

1

INTRODUCTION:
REVELATION REVISITED

I HAVE WRITTEN this chapter as an explanation of those factors which have influenced me in my approach to the writing of this book. As is often the case with academic introductions that discuss methods of study, it might well be preferable to read the primary text of the Book of Revelation first, together with the thematic guide provided by Chapter 2. The reader can then come back to the 'Introduction' last of all, or study it in conjunction with the literary, historical and theological chapters of this Guide.

The act of study is a personal matter. Each of us makes the text her or his own. So I begin with my own personal reactions to the Book of Revelation. In particular I would draw some contrasts between the way I looked at the text in the mid-1960s and the way I perceive it now towards the end of the century. But this is not just a personal matter. The contrasts I draw do also reflect some shifts in the wider academic perspectives on biblical literature over the last 25 years, and the effects that these have on Revelation in particular.

In an earlier book, which I wrote in 1979, I emphasized the importance of understanding the historical context in which Revelation was originally written. Imagery, symbolism and mythology, such as is found in Revelation, can have an almost limitless life-span, and may seem innately volatile. But within a specific religious tradition, such as Jewish and Judaeo-Christian apocalyptic, we can see the same imagery and myth being repackaged and controlled in ways that relate very closely to the political circumstances and religious needs of a particular moment of history, the time of writing of the latest version. This sets before us a quest for the details of ancient history (that is no longer the exclusive preserve of the classicist) and for the history of Early Christianity. In recent years this quest has also been directed to social as well as political history, in a desire to reconstruct what it felt like to live in the world of the New Testament.

There is an irony in the fact that historical interpretation of the Book of Revelation, in the sense of concern with the contemporary history of the time when the book was written, arose rather late in the day, when much of the data for it was already lost. Such historical interpretation of Revelation was motivated in the sixteenth and seventeenth centuries largely as a reaction against those fantastic constructions of world history, cyclical patterns, epochs, or concern for the Millennium, which had dominated exegesis of the Apocalypse in the Middle Ages. But there were some new sources of information to come in the nineteenth and twentieth centuries from archaeology or from the interaction with classical history. These can be seen, for example, when Sir William Ramsay studied the seven letters against their settings in Asia Minor, and Stanislas Giet compared the events of Revelation with the Jewish Revolt and War (66–70 CE), as described by Josephus. But there is an obvious danger, when the evidence is severely limited, that a researcher with special interests will find what he or she wishes to see; historical parallels or coincidences may be identified too easily.

I may already have given the impression, from my personalized approach to the study of Revelation, that I am going to say, 'I used to think as a historian, but now I have changed my mind!' It is true that methods of interpretation seem like changes of fashion, and are usually thought to be mutually exclusive. This has appeared to be especially the case with the historical method, that it seemed incompatible with other options, such as allegorical readings, literary reconstructions, and the comparative studies of religion. But my approach was and is determinedly against such exclusivity. I have wanted to show that we need to take the traditions of mythology seriously, to appreciate the similarities with other religions, the literary manner in which they are presented, and the allegories of theological truth. But like other theological activity, for the author and readers of Revelation these myths were time-bound. We need the historical method to demonstrate how these ideas were particularly related to their contemporary circumstances.

So in what ways have my own perspectives been altered by New Testament scholarship over the last 25 years? I have observed the following areas of change, which I would argue are highly significant, and not just for my personal interpretation of the Book of Revelation:

1. The modern relevance of the ideas of apocalyptic
2. The computerization of criticism
3. Sociological interpretations
4. Images of Empire
5. Literary genres and symbolic structures
6. Readers and the range of their response
7. Wider acceptance of pluralism in method

1. The Modern Relevance of the Ideas of Apocalyptic

H.H. Rowley (*The Relevance of Apocalyptic*, London 1944) and his English-language associates fought a lonely battle to make the apocalyptic literature seem relevant to Christian theology. Only with the 'rediscovery of Apocalyptic' (e.g. Klaus Koch's book of that title, published in Germany in 1970, English translation, London 1972) did German-speaking scholars come to share with their English counterparts a general appreciation of its relevance as a significantly radical strand of Judaism, which had fed into Christian thought. The bizarre world of the Apocalypse might still be dismissed by some as the delusions of a sick nature, but, with the new literary and historical understanding, it would at least be appreciated that the apocalyptist was no psychosomatic case, but had actually been made sick by the evil realities that he was forced to suffer. The Apocalypse thus belongs to the literature of protest and revolt. Or at least that is the emphasis that has spoken most clearly in recent years.

For comparison, we can look back at C.S. Lewis, preaching a

sermon and writing in *The Guardian* in 1942. He is describing the dominance of materialism as the popular creed of
Western Europe:

> For let us make no mistake. If the end of the world appeared in
> all the literal trappings of the Apocalypse, if the modern mate-
> rialist saw with his own eyes the heavens rolled up and the great
> white throne appearing, if he had the sensation of being himself
> hurled into the Lake of Fire, he would continue forever, in that
> lake itself, to regard his experience as an illusion and to find the
> explanation of it in psycho-analysis, or cerebral pathology.
> Experience by itself proves nothing.

In recent decades there has been a much greater willingness
to consider such 'experiences' positively, with a more sympathetic understanding of their context. The book that used to be
regarded as useful only as the script for a horror film came to
be seen as applicable to the Marxist/Socialist view of the twentieth century. In the words of the historian E.J. Hobsbawm,
'We have been taught by the experience of our century to live
in the expectation of apocalypse'. And, as Raymond Williams,
the literary critic, expressed it,

> All the big things, just now, are against us, but within what is
> not only a very powerful but also an exceptionally unstable
> social and cultural order there are forces moving of which
> nobody can depict the outcome.

Since the bombing of Hiroshima, the nuclear threat has been
dominant, and often visualized in terms such as Revelation
16.17-21:

> a violent earthquake, such as had not occurred since people
> were upon the earth, so violent was that earthquake. The great
> city was split into three parts, and the cities of the nations fell...
> And every island fled away and no mountains were to be found.

As Sallie McFague writes, 'the threat of a nuclear holocaust...
[epitomizes] the genuinely novel context in which all con-
structive work in our time, including theology, must take
place' (*Models of God—Theology for an Ecological, Nuclear
Age*, London 1987, p. ix). In recent years other kinds of cosmic
pollution and other abuses of environmental resources have
been recognized as equally life-threatening in the end. 'Green'

campaigners use a mixture of scientific and apocalyptic language in what Jurgen Moltmann called 'the beginning of a life and death struggle for creation on the earth' (*God in Creation*, London 1985, p. xi). The Christian Apocalypse consoles those who glimpse what hell can be, and encourages those who would build a new Jerusalem. Sects (such as Jezreel's Trumpeters) have built Jerusalem to Revelation's ground plan before; what is different now is the scale of the threat and the wider recognition of society's vulnerability. As on the placards proclaiming the end of the world, the text of Revelation is often taken literally, especially by influential fundamentalist groups in the United States of America. The year 1993 saw a most extreme example of this in the Branch Davidian sect, the group led by David Koresh, which immolated itself at the 'Ranch Apocalypse' at Waco in Texas. More positively, in South Africa, Archbishop Desmond Tutu has testified to the power of the vision of Rev. 7.9-12 to uphold him, in the fight against Apartheid. And Chinese Christians used the Apocalypse in the days before Tiananmen Square. Such readings of the text (by literal or allegorical means) are analyzing world conditions by reference to Scripture, not prophesying directly from Scripture like a confident medieval exegete. As in the case of nuclear apocalyptic, comparisons may be simplistic, and may mistake the broadly similar theme for the exactly identical situation; but the text functions as an immediately relevant handling of the issues, not an esoteric code or the fantasies of a disordered brain.

2. The Computerization of Criticism

Literary criticism has been rejuvenated by computer technology. Research projects of a much larger scale, in concordances and analyses of language, grammar and style, can be conceived and carried through without the risk of madness which assailed Alexander Cruden, the pioneer concordance-compiler. Among these new possibilities are the statistical studies of literary style that may assist in the attribution of authorship (e.g. are some or all of the works in the Johannine corpus by

the same author?) or the estimate of a single work's integrity
(in Revelation only ch. 12 was identified as possibly from a
different source, because the statistics were so wildly dis-
crepant). Anthony Kenny set out the principles clearly (in a
THES article summarizing his book):

> The use of stylometry in authorship attribution studies depends
> on the hypothesis that there are quantifiable features of style
> which are characteristic of particular authors. Ideally, a stylo-
> metric test of authorship should be a feature which is charac-
> teristic of all the known works of a particular author and which
> is unique to his works. Features which are to be found in all and
> only the works of a particular author turn out to be frustrat-
> ingly difficult to come by. Authorship attribution problems are
> easier to deal with when they can be cast into the following
> form: in respect of the measured features, does the doubtful
> work resemble the work of candidate author A more than it
> resembles the work of candidate author B?

Studies of language, just as much as studies of an author's
style, can benefit from the enlarged scope and mathematical
precision of computer applications. It was a highlight of an
earlier generation of literary criticism when R.H. Charles
attempted to demonstrate the regularities in the apparently
barbaric Greek of the Apocalypse (see pp. cxvii-clix of the introduction to his ICC commentary on Revelation, Edinburgh
1920). Essentially the author wrote in Greek but thought in
Hebrew. In contrast, G.K. Beale has recently described the
'stylistic use of the Old Testament' in Revelation as 'intentional
solecisms' designed 'to create a "biblical" effect in the hearer'
('Revelation', in *It is Written: Scripture Citing Scripture* (FS
B. Lindars, ed. D.A. Carson and H.M.G. Williamson, Cambridge
1988, p. 332).

Nowadays critics are agreed about very little, beyond the
extent of the general influence of the prophetic literature of
the Old Testament (especially Ezekiel, Isaiah, Jeremiah and
Daniel) upon the author of the Apocalypse. The question to
resolve is one of means: whether that influence is mediated
through classical Hebrew texts, a Greek version (the
Septuagint), or a living language of Aramaic (so that the
Semitic idioms are bilingual with the Greek). This looks like
one exemplification, in the particular text of the Apocalypse,

of a much broader issue, the analysis of the actual nature of 'Biblical Greek' (the term used for the impact of the Old Testament tradition upon Koine Greek). The great need here is for sharper definition (what do we mean by a 'Semitism'? is it clearly distinct from a 'Septuagintalism'?). Wide-ranging relationships of language must be identified and charted, not simply covered by 'umbrella' terms. What the computer offers is the facility to classify and compare examples of grammatical structures, idioms and vocabulary in a precise way in relation to a vast and potentially exhaustive database.

3. Sociological Interpretations

Sociological methods have been employed to interpret available data on the community that produced Revelation. The model frequently employed is that of a sectarian group, marginalized by the attitudes of society. The group is under severe stress, not necessarily overt persecution, but certainly ostracism and social contempt. They feel threatened and insecure, and must also contend with religious stress. Such stress is produced not only by the externally enforced worship of the Roman Emperor, with economic sanctions for non-conformists, but also by some internal conflicts, symbolized in the text of Revelation by the Nicolaitans (2.6, 15) and the synagogue of Satan (2.9). But to speak of sects is not to concentrate entirely on the negative aspects. As Bryan Wilson says, in *The Social Dimensions of Sectarianism: Sects and New Religious Movements in Contemporary Society*, Oxford 1990,

> Sects make a strong reassertion of certain abiding human values, and all of them provide specific grounds for hope in an uncertain world, and offer the occasion for service and self-expression.

For the sociologist of religion, sects are a particularly appropriate and convenient field of research. They are small, clearly defined, self-enclosed communities with relatively fixed belief systems. In the modern world such deviant groups constitute the sharpest of challenges to secularized society, even more than they do to the established religion, from which they are a splinter-group. Care is necessary in transposing this model

to the ancient world. In the case of the varied movements of
early Christianity, which are the representatives of orthodoxy
and of heresy, in the years before the religion is 'established'
in any meaningful sense? On the other hand the inherent
tension between sects and society may be as applicable to the
churches in relation to the Roman Empire as it is in modern
secularism; but the analogy needs to be defended, with careful analysis of the issues.

4. Images of Empire

The title is that of a collection of essays, published in 1991,
and of the conference organized by Loveday Alexander in
Sheffield in March 1990, at which the material was first presented as papers. I use it as a very effective symbol of the
broadly interdisciplinary treatment of the theme of Empire,
which is essential if the sociological model of the sect is to be
sustained.

The programme of the conference was:

> to explore the conflicting images generated by the Roman
> Empire and their afterlife. With the wealth of Roman, Jewish
> and Christian literature at our disposal we have an unparalleled
> opportunity to explore a variety of attitudes to an empire, both
> 'from above' and 'from below'... the wider issues raised by the
> investigation of any well-documented political system from the
> past, and the living force of the images generated in that past
> society. Both the positive and the negative images of the
> Roman Empire have had an influence right through to the
> twentieth century; and successive generations of believers have
> had to wrestle... with the meaning of texts (written under the
> Romans) for a community facing the diverse political realities of
> the twentieth century.

One of the images in the background is that of the four World
Empires found in Daniel and the traditions of Jewish
Apocalyptic. Against this one would set Rome's own self-
generated ideology, which persists to the present day in the
overworked phrase 'the grandeur that was Rome' (borrowed
from Edgar Allan Poe). The basis of this lay in the political
acts and writing of Augustus himself, the promotion of the
imperial cult from the Eastern provinces, the histories of Livy,

and the rhetoric of such as Aelius Aristides. But the view of Rome from within is not entirely harmonious, as can be documented from the writings of Tacitus. The essential contrast between the views of Rome from inside and outside, from above and below, is forcibly presented in the book by Klaus Wengst, *Pax Romana and the Peace of Jesus Christ* (London 1987). His may well be a partisan view; there are certainly other ways of construing some of the texts that Wengst uses. We also need to consider the views of other provincials (e.g. in Asia Minor) and the attitudes of the lowest classes of Roman society (including the slaves) as well as the unusual features of relationships between Rome, the Jews and eventually the Christians.

The tensions between images of Rome persist in the writings of Church Fathers, such as Tertullian and Augustine (particularly in *City of God*). In turn the twentieth century makes its own use of the images of Babylon and the Evil Empire, debates the political appropriateness of Romans 13, and relates Apocalyptic hopes to liberation theology. A further instance is provided by Rainer Stahl, who teaches Old Testament at Leipzig, in a new book (*Von Weltengagement zu Weltüberwindung: Theologische Positionen im Danielbuch*, Kampen, The Netherlands, 1993). He uses the underlying image of 'world empire' from Daniel to interpret modern situations. 'The Russian empire is broken to pieces and has set free Eastern Germany. What can we say about it, having Daniel in mind?'

5. Literary Genres and Symbolic Structures

The method known as Genre Criticism is a significant part of the new literary approaches to the text. The beginnings of genre identification were in Form Criticism with its recognition of formulae (e.g. warnings, macarisms) and of formulaic structures appropriate to particular purposes such as letter-writing. But the study of larger-scale literary genres has now progressed much further, as can be seen in volume 14 of the experimental journal *Semeia*, published in 1979 and dedicated

to explore the morphology of the genre of Apocalypse. The
declared aims (see pp. iii-iv) were:

> to provide a comprehensive survey of all the texts which might
> be or have been classified as apocalypses and can be dated with
> any plausibility in the period 250 BCE—250 CE, with the purpose
> of establishing how far they can purposefully be regarded as
> members of one genre...

> to lend perspective to the view of apocalypses [which in the past
> was based on a few works that were used as the basis for broad
> generalizations] by showing the extent and the limits of the simi-
> larities which are found throughout the apocalyptic corpus...

> to provide perspective on the individual works by which both
> the typical and the distinctive elements can be more fully
> appreciated.

It is a study of the phenomena of the genre, although some
implications for the history of the genre are bound to emerge.

It has long been recognized that the Book of Revelation is
an amalgam of literary types, even allowing for a single
authorship of the final work. In the past the variety has been
used by critics in order to discriminate, for example favouring
the letters to the seven churches in chs. 2 and 3, but despising
their apocalyptic packaging. Recent study of the component
parts of Revelation may not be so partisan, but has often
resulted in a battle between the genres. Is the dominant type
that of the letters, or are they merely an epistolary frame for
communications that more closely resemble imperial edicts?
Given such an imperial perspective, with its political dimension so important in modern interpretation, is the setting of
chs. 4 and 5 modelled on the Emperor's audience chamber?
The dominant genre is then Roman imperial court ceremonial
which is here so effectively parodied. Does this mean we must
reject the influential interpretation in terms of a heavenly
liturgy, which itself is a projection of the liturgical forms and
practice of the early Church? (See Gregory Dix, *The Shape of
the Liturgy* 1945[2] p. 28). Or is the character of Revelation
essentially dramatic, as a literary form 'meant to be read
aloud', indeed to be performed as a combination of liturgical
and theatrical experience? Recognition of such a genre would
entail that we picture the twenty-four elders in the heavenly

transformation of a Greek theatre, with God's throne and Christ as the Lamb on stage.

There is equal diversity among the schools of literary structuralism, which sought to explain, from the organizational principles and apparently self-conscious structures of the text, the nature of the symbolic universe that was constructed or reflected in this book. If one can speak of this 'universe' in terms of Realism, then it can be conceived as a response to their social world, made by the group to which the author belongs, a group that may well be on the margins. One can hardly expect any single diagram on a printed page to do justice to the structure of this text, let alone this universe. One needs to think in terms of interlocking facets in a three-dimensional figure. Structuralism invites some reconsideration of traditional interpretations, such as the theories of recapitulation. It should not be assumed that the order of Revelation is chronological, rather than thematically and theologically conceived. The combination of linear narrative with repetitions and celebrations in the form of hymns can reveal a deliberate intention to set up tensions in the structure, for rhetorical effect. The resulting overall shape of this chiastic work has been likened to the geometric figure of a conic spiral by Elizabeth Schüssler Fiorenza (*The Book of Revelation, Justice and Judgment*).

6. Readers and the Range of their Response

To talk exclusively of author's intention (even if collectively expressed of the author's community) would be regarded as unforgivably one-sided in terms of the modern approach to a literary text. There is need to leave room for all that happens to a text after it leaves the author's hands. In the case of the biblical tradition there is an extremely rich vein of interpretation, up to and including modern preaching, apologetic, and literary reading. Even in the historical context in which the text was first produced there is room to consider the earliest stages of audience interaction with the text. What impression did the author hope to make? Can we tell if he succeeded in whole or in part? Even without regarding it as a theatrical script for performance, are there signs that a text has been modified by audience participation?

In the opening vision of Revelation 1, there is a call narrative which underlines the authority of the writer and legitimates the activity of this Christian prophet. To see how vital is this initial emphasis, one can ask what would be lost if the Apocalypse began, as it obviously could, with 1.9. The text has undeniable importance in a struggle for power. The Christian prophet is asserting the dominion of Jesus as King over against the blasphemous pretensions of the Emperor to set himself up as God (in his imperial edicts). But might the power struggle also be internal as well as external to this Christian community? The book begins as it does because the author knows that the voice of his prophecy has been and will be contested by other Christians. Against this threat to his authority John attests his own direct commissioning and deliberately allows his narrative voice to merge with the words of angels and of Christ himself.

A larger literary structure than any discussed so far is the ultimate canon of scripture of the Old and New Testaments which concludes with the Book of Revelation. Defining the limits of canon so as to include Revelation, after protracted disputes about it in the church, is an example of large-scale reader response that needs to be discussed in historical terms. But exponents of canonical criticism insist that the sweep of material 'from Moses to Patmos' should be evaluated in literary and theological terms. How may we best describe the climax to the canon which this last book represents? But if the literary model of the Old Testament 'canon' is at all influential in the arrangement of the New Testament, we may have to conclude that Revelation, like Daniel and the works of the Chronicler among the 'Writings', is more appendix than climax.

7. Conclusions:
Wider Acceptance of Pluralism in Method

The contrast between the older and newer approaches is most marked as Revelation is applied to Christian preaching. Not so long ago typical selections for sermons were the glimpses of early Christian behaviour in the seven letters, and the comforting passages used at funerals. Now the focus is on political, social and environmental threats, and the themes of responsibility, justice, judgment and vengeance. The book becomes a study of power, also raising ethical issues about responses to power at a time of crisis. Revelation functions as a warning to the complacent within society, or has a cathartic effect on the community by arousing intense feelings of inflammatory aggressiveness. Or it may be a moral lesson on the victim's desire for vengeance. How can one decide which function is most appropriate, most true to the original situation of the writer?

Some refuse to see the book as relative to any one situation in particular, but rather as timeless and therefore valid for all times. Just as allegorical exegesis emphasizes the moment of interpretation as much as, if not more than, the moment of writing, so a modern hermeneutic theory insists that the meaning of a work is primarily what it means to the reader. Pluralism of method can turn into an ideological pluralism in which there are no objectively correct answers, only a range of subjective responses. There may be a heady sense of freedom about such interpretation, but it is difficult to pose questions of original or ultimate truth. The contributions of the author and of his situation to what is said—and the ways in which this handles, and is handled by, the continuity of traditions—must still retain some significance, if not decisive control, in questions of meaning.

Revelation is a relevant text for many crises. But the intoxication of a theme like Justice and Judgment should not blind one to the balance of other issues in the book. Literature rich in imagery and symbolism deserves to be studied as a work of art, in the light of the great works of art (e.g. paintings) that it has inspired. And Revelation's vision of an alternative world derives power from the actual contrast with the socio-political realities that gave it birth. For literary tensions and theological dialectic to be understood fully, historical questions must remain part of the interpreter's task. To appreciate the apocalyptic traditions that feed into the book, and the theological, sectarian and monastic traditions that are fed by it,

Revelation's place in the story must be located and illumi-
nated. The 'new look' at Revelation produced by both structural and sociological analyses is welcome, precisely because it
contributes to a fuller reading of the book and of the circumstances that produced it. The real need is for a total view, to
interrelate methods and results and demonstrate Revelation's
lasting contribution to the Christian tradition.

2
READING REVELATION
BY THEMES

Outline Chart of the Book of Revelation

1.1-3   Introduction as to an apocalyptic work

1.4-8   Introduction as to a circular letter to the Asian churches

1.9-20   John's heavenly vision of Christ as the Son of Man

2, 3   Seven particular letters to seven existing churches (associated with the author) in Asia Minor

4, 5   John's vision of worship in the royal throne-room of heaven; Christ as the Lamb receives the sealed book of prophecy

6   Christ opens six of the seven seals: the realities of the present and of recent history (e.g. war and famine) are interpreted as symbols of prophecy

7   Heavenly interlude:
         the sealing of those who are to be spared
         the worship by those called to be saints

8, 9   The seventh seal:
         silence and liturgy
         six of the seven trumpet blasts portending disasters

10   Interlude:
         the mighty angel
         the seven thunders are suppressed
         the prophet John receives (and inwardly digests) a scroll

11   The contents of this scroll (a flash-back, to interpret
          past history):
                the fall of Jerusalem to the Romans (67–70 CE)
                the model provided by Peter and Paul of apostolic
                    witness to Christ (64–67 CE)
          The seventh trumpet sounds amid heavenly worship

12, 13   The seventh trumpet heralds the disastrous arrival
          on earth of the two beasts (13.1, 11)
          The portent of the woman with the child (12) supplies
          the context: the diabolical beasts are on earth because
          the devil was expelled from heaven (12.9); and this
          expulsion was a consequence of Christ's incarnation
          and resurrection. So the church on earth is persecuted
          (12.17)

14   The song of the saints in heaven
          Angelic proclamations of judgment on earth
          Harvest and winepress as symbols of God's judgment

15   Heavenly interlude, as the seven bowls of wrath are
          introduced

16   The bowls contain plagues (like the plagues of Egypt
          at the time of the Exodus) which are the judgment of
          God's wrath upon the earth (and what the beasts
          have brought about there)

17   The Roman Empire (particularly the blasphemy of
          worshipping the Emperor as divine) is to be destroyed
          in God's judgment

18   Warnings of the fall of Imperial Rome, and the
          lamentations of those (merchants and clients) affected
          by her fall

19   Song of triumph in heaven
          Anticipation of the marriage of Christ, the Lamb
          Christ rides forth victorious to the last battle

20   The Millennium (the thousand-year reign of Christ
          and the saints)
          The final resurgence of the powers of evil
          The Last Judgment

21.1–
22.5   The vision of the heavenly city, New Jerusalem (the
       church in heaven as the bride of Christ)
       The new created order—the paradise garden

22.6-20 Final guarantees and solemn warnings, appropriate
       to an apocalyptic work (see 1.1-3)
       Christ's second coming is imminent

22.21 Ending appropriate to a letter (see 1.4-8)

Introduction

According to Etienne Charpentier (*How to Read the New
Testament*, London 1982, p. 105), 'the Book of Revelation, the
Apocalypse, is a book of fire and blood in the image of our
world'. This view suggests a sense of realism and of urgent
relevance, just as some people have found that experience of
wartime or of nuclear catastrophe sends them back to these
words of prophecy. A few readers are confident, in an almost
proprietorial way, about the meaning of the book and how it
relates to them in their present situation. Most people are
much less sure and may not even know where to begin (or
whether they want to begin!). Some readers may even doubt
whether this book deserves to be in the New Testament at all.

In such circumstances the most important question is how
one should read the book. There are three main things to
consider:

1. We must be aware of the situation in which the book
    came into being: in a small Christian group, politically
    vulnerable and persecuted for its faith.

2. It must be read imaginatively, in a way that is
    responsive to the writer's images and use of symbolism:
    this means enjoying the sound of the words them-
    selves and relating the verbal pictures to the reader's
    memory of the Old Testament and of Christian art.

3. Perhaps most importantly, we must recognize the
    author's theological priorities: the relationships of this

world to the world to come, and of the church to the crucified and risen Lord, and of the Son to the Father who is the world's creator—all these are vital connections in the structure of the Apocalypse.

I suggest we study a selection of passages, arranged thematically into five sequences, which pick up these theological priorities. In this way it is possible to see a relationship between sequence A, Visions of God; sequence B, Visions of the Church in the World; sequence C, Visions of Creation and the End of the Universe; sequence D, Visions of Rival Powers; and sequence E, Visions of Future Hope. This is not to stop your reading the book straight through from start to finish. But perhaps this can best be done subsequently, following the outline chart of the book that precedes this chapter, and in the light of the thematic perspectives which I am now going to indicate.

A. Visions of God

A.1. *Revelation 1.12-16: The Son of Man*
Many are the faces of Christ in Christian art through the centuries and in different parts of the world. Even in a single time and place there may be contrasting features. In the dominant image of Christ as 'all powerful' in the Byzantine cathedrals, some representations are of a fierce judge, others are benevolent, with hand lifted in blessing.

Christ as the Son of Man in heavenly glory—this is the face of Christ that John sees in his first vision. We know that the heavenly Son of Man was an important image of Christ for the early Christians. The gospels refer to the Son of Man in three different ways. He has power on earth, with authority to forgive sins (Mk 2.10) and as Lord of the Sabbath (Mk 2.28). He is the one who is destined to suffer rejection and betrayal and to be condemned to death (Mk 8.31; 9.31; 10.33-34). And it is the Son of Man, prophesied at a time of trial, who is 'seated at the right hand of the Power, and "coming with the clouds of heaven"' (Mk 14.62). The early Christians were familiar with the picture in Dan. 7.13-14 ('I saw one like a son of man coming with the clouds of heaven. And he came to the

Ancient of Days and was presented before him. To him was given dominion and glory and kingship'). They saw this prophecy fulfilled in Jesus who had shared their earthly conditions and sufferings and was vindicated through resurrection after a cruel death. The relationship of suffering to triumph, demonstrated in Jesus, was a source of great encouragement to Christians experiencing hardship.

In John's vision of the heavenly Son of Man there is a mixture of elements from Old Testament pictures (Ezek. 1, Dan. 7, and Moses in Exod. 34). It is an image of great power and glory, both judgmental (the 'sharp, two-edged sword') and intensely reassuring (1.17). The author is commissioned to write what he sees for the benefit of the Christian churches. They are the seven stars and lampstands and so they are already part of the picture. This vision of the glorious figure of Christ is for their benefit. And when the individual churches are addressed in the letters, particular features of the description of the Son of Man are directly called to mind (e.g. 1.16 in 2.12).

A.2. *Revelation 1.17-20: Death and Life*
Stephen, the first Christian martyr, according to Acts 7, has a vision of heaven before he is stoned to death.

> But filled with the Holy Spirit, he gazed into heaven and saw the glory of God and Jesus standing at the right hand of God. 'Look,' he said, 'I see the heavens opened and the Son of Man standing at the right hand of God!' (7.55-56).

The most distinctive feature of Stephen's vision is that the Son of Man is *standing*, rather than traditionally sitting at the right hand of God. What effect does this have? It emphasizes the immediacy of the contact between Jesus and this man who is to die for the name of Christ. Christ stands ready to come, ready for his triumphal second coming, at the point of Stephen's death.

In Revelation we have seen the close connection between the churches and the heavenly vision. The Christian communities are in difficulties and the vision of Christ the Son of Man in glory will sustain them. But this works for isolated individuals as well as for beleaguered groups and churches.

To the church in Laodicea, the risen Christ is described as 'the Amen, the faithful and true witness, the origin of God's creation' (3.14). This is a marvellous description, combining the depth of understanding of the person of Christ (as in Col. 1.15-20 and Jn 1) with the richness of early Christian worship and the beginnings of the liturgy. But the centrepiece is Christ as the faithful *witness* (*martus* is the Greek word which starts by meaning 'witness' and, as a consequence of the persecutions of early Christianity, finishes by meaning 'martyr' as well).

Stephen, the martyr, faced a death in the image of Christ's death. For Christ is the true witness who experienced death in obedience to God. The individual Christian in the seven churches is in the same position. There is a particular example referred to in the church at Pergamum: 'Antipas my witness, my faithful one, who was killed among you, where Satan lives' (2.13). We know nothing of the circumstances of this death. But we know that it was early Christian belief that by such a death a disciple perfectly followed his or her Lord. And earthly disciple and heavenly Lord were united in this moment.

A.3. *Revelation 4.1-8: The Throne of God*

> Before the main hall was an ante-room where those waiting sat on raised stone benches along the walls. There was a stone basin in the centre, which contained water for washing the hands (a symbolic purification of the whole body). From this room there was access to the audience chamber itself, where the king received visitors, flanked by his counsellors and priests on more raised benches. In the centre of the northern wall is the superb throne made of gypsum on which the king himself sat. On the wall above and on each side of the throne is a fresco representing griffins (with head of eagle and body of lion) symbolizing the earthly and heavenly powers of the king.

This is a description of the palace of king Minos at Knossos on Crete, claimed to be the oldest throne and audience chamber in the world. But for representative symbols of power it can be matched by the palace of the Persian kings at Persepolis, by the Peacock throne in the Hall of Private Audience (Diwan-i-Khas) in the Red Fort at Delhi, or even by the chair of St

Augustine at the east end of Canterbury Cathedral. John's vision in Revelation stands between the symbols of ancient political power in the East and their reinterpretation as spiritual power in the great liturgies and architecture of the Christian church. David E. Aune has argued for a more particular relationship: 'John's description of the heavenly ceremonial practiced in the throne room of God bears such a striking resemblance to the ceremonial of the [Roman] imperial court and cult that the latter can only be a parody of the former' ('The Influence of Roman Imperial Court Ceremonial on the Apocalypse of John', *Papers of the Chicago Society of Biblical Research* 27, 1983, p. 5).

It is certainly important to see John's description within an ongoing tradition. The threefold acclamation of holiness (4.8) goes back to Isaiah's vision in the temple (Isa. 6.3) and leads on to the *Trishagion* or *Sanctus* ('Holy, Holy, Holy') in the Christian liturgy (cf. 1 Clem. 34.6). The wording in Revelation is actually closer to later liturgies than to the Septuagint translation of Isaiah. The four living creatures around the throne (4.6) reflect the vision of God in Ezek. 1.5-28 and in turn are the basis for the much later Christian symbols for the Four Evangelists (lion, ox, man, eagle). And the twenty-four elders, seated like the presbyters round the bishop, or the advisers beside the monarch—do they represent for John the angelic host, or the Christian saints, or the patriarchs and other worthy figures of the Old Testament? Like the statues at Chartres Cathedral, the figures of both Old and New Testaments come together, flanking the centrepiece of the vision, the inexpressible majesty of almighty God.

A.4. *Revelation 5.1-6: The Lamb of God*
There is a vivid Flemish painting by the brothers Hubert and Jan van Eyck, an altarpiece completed in 1432 and now in the cathedral church of St Bavon in Ghent, Belgium. The inscription reads, 'Hubert van Eyck, the most famous painter ever known, started this work of art...his brother Jan, who was the second in art, finished the momentous commission... Admire now what they have done for you.' The Lamb of God is the main subject of the painting, sometimes referred to as

The Adoration of the Mystic Lamb. The setting is a landscape,
the paradise garden seen in northern European terms. A host
of worshippers—burghers, ladies, friars and ecclesiastics—
come from all four corners of the picture. In the centre a ring
of angels surrounds an altar with a red frontal on which
stands the figure of the Lamb. The glory of God radiates over
the landscape from a light source in which the dove as the
spirit of God is represented, and out of a fountain in the
foreground come the streams of the water of life.

It should be with some surprise that the Lamb of God is first
seen in John's vision of the continuing heavenly worship
around God's throne. A legally sealed and witnessed document
contains a statement of what is to happen to the world. But
nobody is found worthy to open the document, except Jesus
Christ himself. The Seer affirms that Christ is the descendant
of David, whose kingdom in Judaea traced its origins back to
the sons of Jacob. Jacob called Judah his son 'a lion's whelp'
(Gen. 49.9). So the Messiah, the son of David, can be called
the Lion of the tribe of Judah. But when the Christ, who is
found worthy, is seen, he appears not as a lion but as a lamb.

Christ is the 'Lamb standing, as though it had been slain'.
He bears the marks of his suffering and death, though he
stands by the throne of God in his risen glory. It is in his
death that his victory is achieved; as conqueror he can reveal
the future, for he sees with the spiritual eyes of God into all
parts of the earth (5.6). These ideas are represented also in
the van Eyck altarpiece. The spiritual light of God pervades
every part of the picture. And the Lamb stands on the altar
alongside a chalice of his blood; the altar frontal is red, the
liturgical colour for martyrdom. From this comes the confidence that 'the Lamb will conquer them, for he is Lord of lords
and King of kings' (17.14).

A.5. *Revelation 5.7-14: The Lamb of God*
John stressed the uniqueness of Christ in an unfamiliar way.
He alone has been found worthy to open the scroll. When
Paul describes the uniqueness of Christ, it is in relation to
universal sinfulness ('There is no one who is righteous, not
even one', Rom. 3.10). Jesus Christ is the sole righteous person,

suffering innocently in his death. For Paul the death of Christ deals with sin and enables Christians, baptized into his death, to be united with Christ in resurrected life (Rom. 6.3-11). John uses very different words, but his concentration on the uniqueness of Christ's sacrificial death is essentially complementary to that of Paul.

The Lamb of God is clearly an image of sacrifice, reminiscent of the lamb which is sacrificed at the Jewish Passover (Exod. 12). In later years each Jewish family sacrificed a lamb at the temple. So Paul could recall this in describing the death of Jesus as a Passover sacrifice (1 Cor. 5.7). And, according to John's Gospel, John the Baptist draws attention to Jesus as 'the Lamb of God who takes away the sin of the world' (Jn 1.29). But this idea of sacrifice does not work purely in terms of Jewish practice, because neither the Passover lamb nor the lamb of the daily burnt offering was intended to atone for sins. Perhaps we need to refer to the suffering Servant, in Isa. 53.7, 12 described as 'a lamb that is led to the slaughter' who 'bore the sins of many'. But the most important part of the definition of the Lamb as an image of sacrifice is the action of Christ himself in dying on the cross; the rest is interpretation.

The great paradox is that the victim (the Lamb) functions as the leader (the Lion and the Shepherd) in Rev. 5.5 and 14.1-7. There may be a precedent for this in the Jewish apocalyptic *Book of Enoch* where David is represented as a lamb who becomes the ram and leader of the flock (89.46). In the next chapter one of the sheep sprouts a great horn, and he becomes the victorious bell-wether of God's flock, as does the messianic figure in *Testament of Joseph* 19.8. Possibly this ram was already a familiar idea in apocalyptic circles. But let us not forget that the power of John's statement lies in the paradoxical combination of strength and weakness. 'The Lamb bore the marks of slaughter…with his life-blood he had ransomed for God men from every tribe, tongue, people and race. The Lamb is the symbol of self-sacrificing and redemptive love' (Caird, *Revelation*, p. 74).

A.6. *Revelation 15.2-8: The Old Testament Vision of God*
With this vision we are taken back into the audience chamber

or sanctuary of heaven; it is both the palace of God and the
temple for his worshippers. Among the furnishings of the
throne room, which we have seen before, the focus of attention is on 'a sea of glass, like crystal' (4.6). Its origins are probably in the 'sea' of cast bronze in Solomon's temple (1 Kgs
7.23), a symbol of the cosmos (the ocean of chaos transformed
by God in creation mythology). Now the cosmos reflects a fiery
red, whether the fire of the judgment which is coming, or the
colour of blood, shed in the sacrifice of Christ's martyrs who
now worship in the presence of God. For the congregation has
increased beyond the four living creatures and the twenty-
four elders. It now comprises the one hundred and forty-four
thousand servants of God who were selected and sealed (7.4-
8) and have now been resurrected from the earth (14.1-5), to
sing God's praise to the accompaniment of harp music.

The song of praise is ascribed first to Moses. It is striking
how much of the chapter's symbolism recalls the Exodus: the
plagues of Egypt (Exod. 7–11); the way through the Red Sea
(Exod. 14); the song which Moses and the Israelites sing
(Exod. 15); the tent of meeting and the cloud of smoke which
prevents entry (Exod. 40.35; cf. the smoke in Isa. 6.4). The
conquerors celebrate their victory just as the Israelites
celebrated their crossing of the sea. The crossing of the Red
Sea stands for the martyrdom of the victors and their crossing
over into God's presence through death. And yet the song of
praise is also ascribed to the Lamb, because those victories
were only achieved through Christ and his sacrifice. The
words of the song are a skilful amalgam of Old Testament
quotations. It sums up the Old Testament vision of God, as the
King to whom all nations come (Mic. 4.1-3). This could be
regarded by Israel in a rather nationalistic way (Isa. 49.22-23;
60.10-16). But in Revelation the martyrs express a confidence
in *universal* salvation, of which they are the 'first fruits'.

The rest of the chapter reminds the reader of two essentially
complementary aspects: the God of justice for Israel and the
world is the God of wrath, who executes his judgment with
righteous anger and authorizes the plagues with power.
Again the comparison is with Moses and the plagues on
Egypt. This is no doctrine of God as a petty tyrant, but rather

of God as ultimately in control of all creation. As G.B. Caird wrote: 'The proof of God's ultimate sovereignty is that he can use even the powers of evil to be the means of their own destruction' (p. 197).

A.7. *Revelation 19.11-16: The Rider on the White Horse*
Everybody knows of the four horsemen of the Apocalypse, the riders on white, red, black and pale horses (Rev. 6.2-8; see also sequence D.1 below). They represent major threats to the first-century Mediterranean world: death and destruction from warfare, famine and pestilence. It is likely that the first rider, the warlike figure on the white horse, represents the conquering power of one of the new religious movements (mystery religions). Mithraism (the cult of Mithras) spread from Persia throughout the Roman empire. It was associated with the armed forces of Parthia and the Roman legions and it spread rapidly wherever those armies went. While everybody knows the symbols of four horsemen, comparatively few are aware of the much more powerful figure, the bloodstained rider of ch. 19.

We have already seen how John achieves a dramatic effect by contrast and paradox, in the figure of the Lamb of God. This rider is another image of Christ, as the bloodstained robe, the title 'the Word of God' (19.13), and the acclamation 'Faithful and True' (19.11 recalling 3.14), all make clear. Other features such as 'eyes...like a flame of fire' and 'from his mouth...a sharp sword', recall the vision of the heavenly Son of Man in Revelation 1. The accompanying armies of heaven, dressed in pure white linen and also riding white horses, are those who have conquered with Christ (7.14) and follow the leadership of the Lamb (14.1-7). Their celibacy recalls the ideals of the Qumran community.

This vision is set in deliberate contrast to that of the first rider. The way of Christ is declared superior to the way of Mithras and the mystery cults and more powerful than the might of the Roman legions. On Christ's head are 'many diadems' (19.12), in contrast to the limited number of crowned heads among the adverse powers of the beast and the dragon. The title of Christ's victory is inscribed where his sword of

judgment would normally hang (19.16) and also on his blood-
soaked garment. With the same kind of artistic contrast in
mind, Franz Marc and Wassily Kandinsky coined the term
'Blue Rider' in 1911 for their new movement in modern art,
based on exuberant colour and profound emotions. Blue is
associated with the other-worldly and spiritual, because it is
rarely found in nature except as the colour of the sky. In contrast to the Horsemen of the Apocalypse, bearers of devastation and death, the paradoxical formula of the Blue Rider
stands for spiritual renewal pitted against spiritual despair.
While Kandinsky in an earlier phase had depicted Cossack
riders, Marc now painted a group of heroic horses in the
imagery of paradise. The desired result was a positive programme of spiritual harmony; he said in the prospectus for
the 1912 Almanac: 'we stand before the new pictures as in a
dream and we hear the apocalyptic [revelatory] horsemen in
the air'.

One other feature of the context of Revelation 19 deserves
more attention than it is usually given. A marriage is
announced at 19.7, 9; but it does not take place until the
arrival of the bride at 21.2. This theme of wedding celebration
absorbs the Old Testament idea of a great feast at the end of
time symbolizing God's kingdom (e.g. Isa. 25.6). The same
connection is made in some of the Royal Psalms in the Psalter,
especially Psalm 45 (the Royal Wedding Psalm), where the joy
of the celebration and the beauty of the royal bride are
depicted, and the bridegroom is introduced:

> You are the most handsome of men… Gird your sword on your
> thigh, O mighty one, in your glory and majesty. In your majesty
> ride on victoriously for the cause of truth and to defend the right;
> let your right hand teach you dread deeds.

Here is a prototype of Revelation's imagery: the wedding of
the warrior-king who rides in triumph. If this wedding is
announced in ch. 19 and solemnized in ch. 21, it could mean
that the intervening ch. 20 is concerned with who will, and
who will not, receive wedding invitations (see sequence D.7
below)

Summary of Sequence A: Visions of God

John sees visions and is commissioned to communicate them to the churches. Are they real visions, or artistic creations, or a mixture of the two? John's writing faithfully reflects the range of thought of early Christians about the majesty of God the Creator of the world, and about the person of Jesus Christ,

> the Son of Man
> the faithful witness to God
> the Lamb of God
> now vindicated and victorious.

We must not underestimate the depth of theological awareness that underlies these dramatic visions. For Christian believers, to see Christ in this way generates a tremendous confidence and trust in God's salvation, whatever the future may hold.

B. Visions of The Church in the World

B.1. *Revelation 1.1-11: The Lord's Day*
After the prologue (vv. 1-3), which describes the nature of the Revelation, the book begins all over again in the form of a letter. The opening greetings exactly follow the standard pattern with which we are familiar from the letters of Paul. We know a great deal about the early church from those letters which Paul addressed to particular named churches. It is possible to imagine how each letter, when it arrived, would be read aloud to the congregation at its regular meeting (cf. 1 Thess. 5.27; Col. 4.16). In this way the writer could speak quite directly to the whole local church gathered in the context of worship.

It is reasonable to suppose that John saw his first vision as if in a local meeting of the church community. 'I was in the Spirit on the Lord's day' (1.10). If John was not actually in the meeting, because of the circumstances of solitary exile on Patmos, then he imagined himself back with one of the church communities on the Asian mainland. We can hardly exclude the possibility of an actual ecstatic experience of physical translation (see Ezek. 3.12; 2 Cor. 12.2). For the suggestion of Christian meetings on the first day of the week, Revelation should be compared with Jn 20.19, 26; Acts 20.7 and 1 Cor. 16.2 (see also *Did.* 14.1; Ignatius, *Magn.* 9.1. 'Of Jewish origin...is the seven-day week, and the weekly day of worship which the Church soon transferred from the sabbath to Sunday, the day of the Resurrection' (T. Klauser, *A Short History of the Western Liturgy* Oxford 1979², p. 6). By the time of Justin Martyr in the mid second century CE, the Sunday assembly for word and sacrament had become conventional (see *1 Apology* 65–67). It is worth noting that while the Jewish sabbath (Saturday) was kept as a day of rest, and many people now regard Saturday and Sunday alike as the 'weekend', the innovative Christian choice of Sunday to celebrate the Resurrection ('the Lord's day') meant gathering for the eucharist at a very early hour on a normal working day.

The influence of Sunday worship is strong in the Apocalypse. We have little hard evidence about any standard patterns in the earliest Christian worship. But it is an attractive speculation that in the many hymns of Revelation, the heavenly songs of praise, worship and thanksgiving, we can trace the instincts of the early Christian community. If so, then certainly the human words are transfigured into the glorious songs of the angels and saints in heaven. These words then came to be used in the later Christian liturgies, thus completing the circle. According to Revelation the worship of earth and heaven is drawn together in unanimous paeans of praise.

> To the one seated on the throne and to the Lamb be blessing
> and honour and glory and might for ever and ever! (Rev. 5.13)

B.2. *Revelation 2.1-7: The Church in Ephesus*

In the foundations of Rochester Cathedral in Kent the crypt, constructed in Early English style, is arranged in seven aisles, originally housing seven chapels, to symbolize the seven churches of the Apocalypse. The original seven churches were actual centres of Christianity in Asia Minor—not the only seven, of course, for that would be to disregard other centres visited by St Paul. These seven in Revelation are chosen for

practical reasons: they were probably centres of the Johannine
mission field—perhaps the only churches acknowledging
John—and they are also linked, for purposes of communication, by the imperial post road that circumscribes the west-
central region of the province of Asia. But they are also the
first of the book's symbolic sequences of sevens, symbols of the
whole Church, foundations of Christendom, and as such
figure, with their guardian angels, as the stars and lampstands of the opening vision (1.12-20). In the Early Church
references to angels are intriguing, but angelology is not an
exact science. As Stuart G. Hall writes, 'Jesus Christ's own self-
manifestation to a prophet may be called an angel' (*Doctrine
and Practice in the Early Church*, London 1991, p. 55)

The message to Ephesus stands first and foremost among
the seven dictated letters and the seven churches. Ephesus
was the port of entry, regularly used by the Roman governor
arriving in the province; it was the commercial centre and
chief city of Roman Asia. (Only Sardis, the ancient capital of
Lydia, has a similar status symbol in the opening reference of
its letter.) The allusions to the opening vision (2.1; 3.1; 1.12-
13, 16) are not random selections, but symbols appropriate to
the location. For the seer, the true Church is centred on Christ
himself; theologically this is far more significant than the
representative character or political pretensions of the local
'centre'. The threat to 'remove your lampstand' (2.5) is both a
symbol of this judgment and an allusion to the history of
Ephesus as one of movement. The site of the city had to be
changed (c. 550 and again c. 287 BCE) because the naviga-
bility of its harbour was threatened by the silting up of the
river Cayster. Theological threats and promises thus can be
seen to satirize the local environment of the church. Both
'tree' and 'paradise' (2.7) are echoes of Genesis 2–3, but also
parodies of the tree-shrine of Artemis (Diana) at Ephesus and
of its sacred enclosure which offered asylum.

There are indications of clear religious opposition in Ephesus
(false apostles—2.2; Nicolaitans—2.6) but their identities are
far from clear. We have already noted the likelihood of
internal religious tensions, as well as external 'persecution' in
these churches. The Johannine communities may still sustain

a prophetic type of ministry, just as the seer himself is a Christian prophet with ecstatic experiences (1.10). If so, the church organization would differ radically from that which is known elsewhere in Asia Minor. And there could be rival prophets to John, such as 'Balaam' and 'Jezebel' (2.15, 20), just as the prophets of ancient Israel experienced contradiction (cf. 1 Kgs 22). But care is needed because there is little evidence on which to identify these local opponents, or even associate them together. Perhaps it is most plausible that they should be pro-government collaborators (like Israel's false prophets) rather than other apocalyptic prophets more radical than John himself. The irony is that Balaam originally represented the kind of prophet who could not be bought (Num. 22–24; ctr. 31.16).

B.3. *Revelation 3.14-22: The Church in Laodicea*

Laodicea is the last of the seven representative churches to be addressed. It serves as a particular example of how all the unsatisfactory features of a local church situation are vividly depicted. As we saw in the previous sequence the church is addressed by the risen Christ, here named as 'the Amen, the faithful and true witness' (3.14). This is the standard by which the local Christians can and should be measuring themselves.

Laodicea does not emerge as conspicuously faithful. The description suggests a resourceful, successful and perhaps rather self-satisfied community which lacks spiritual depth. John's picture contains references to the local features of this city in the Lycus valley, neighbour to Colossae and Hierapolis. He uses the local references to make a telling spiritual commentary on the church. The quality of the local water supply was a famous joke; it was brought five miles by aqueduct, warmed up by the sun. Colossae had cold pure water and Hierapolis hot medicinal springs. Laodicea is actually criticised for its ineffectiveness, with water no use for anything—not for being half-hearted, which is the usual sense in which the proverbial lukewarmness is understood today. The city stood at the crossroads, controlling the trade routes. This makes the door or gate (3.20) especially significant. Laodicea went in for an ostentatious building programme after the earthquake in

60 CE, with a monumental triple gate to the city. As a trading city it was the centre for banking. One local speciality was cloth woven from the raven-black wool of local sheep. The medical school was renowned for its eye-specialists; a 'Phrygian powder' (an eyesalve made from alum) was widely used. All these features are combined in a symbolic description of the church as measured by its risen Lord. It may have appeared notably successful to others, but was itself blind to its own spiritual ineffectiveness. The emphasis in the conclusion is upon the individual and voluntary action. As Colin J. Hemer wrote, the Christian needs

> the fellowship of Christ in the present as the antidote to the self-sufficiency of a Christless church. Christ would not abuse and exploit hospitality as Roman potentates did. Only with the personal presence of Christ would [the Christian] conquer (*The Letters to the Seven Churches*, p. 207).

B.4. *Revelation 1.5-6; 5.9-10: The Priesthood*

These two texts are often taken out of Revelation as proofs of the idea of the priesthood of the whole people of God, the priesthood of all believers. They are combined with 1 Pet. 2.9: 'But you are a chosen race, a royal priesthood, a holy nation, God's own people, in order that you may proclaim the mighty acts of him who called you out of darkness into his marvelous light'. These texts are applying to the church language from the Old Testament about the people of Israel (see Exod. 19.5-6). Of course historic Israel had a quite narrowly defined and institutional priesthood, and a charismatic experience of individual prophecy that could on occasion condemn the priesthood, as well as this wider vision of national vocation and purpose.

I have already referred to theories about the nature of ministry (prophetic or priestly) implied in Revelation. What is clear from the context of this quotation in the Apocalypse is that, for the Seer, the priestly function of the people of God depends upon the self-sacrificial act of Christ. God's people are ransomed for God, freed from their sins, by the blood of Christ. Kenneth Mason writes:

All the New Testament ideas about priesthood are rooted in an
inchoate but vivid intuition of natural and universal human
priesthood—a potential priesthood of every man and woman...
The institutional priesthoods which society develops have to be
seen as an admission of failure. It is as though the consecration
of human life has to be acted out in show because it is not
achieved in reality. If that is so then the various references in
the New Testament to priesthood can be read as claims to the
restoration of that reality through the work of Christ...
Revelation had shown that priesthood and sacrifice found their
fulness in Christ crucified (*Priesthood and Society*, Norwich
1992, pp. 39, 55).

We can conclude that for believers any kind of Christian
ministry or sacrificial act depends ultimately upon the action
of Christ as priest and victim, even if the precise nature of the
sacramental theology varies with situation and time.

But there is a further dimension that Revelation empha-
sises. As a 1986 Church of England report on the ordained
priesthood has said:

The final chapters of the Revelation to John present a picture of
the fulfilment of all things in which the whole company of the
redeemed serve God face to face. Part of this picture is that
there will be no more temple (Revelation 21.22): God will be
immediately present to his people. In other words, there will be
no more need for sacraments or priests to mediate God's presence. Thus, whereas those who are redeemed by Christ will be
kings and priests for ever, the priesthood of the ordained ministry belongs to the realm which is passing away (*The
Priesthood of the Ordained Ministry*, Board of Mission and Unity,
Westminster 1986, p. 101).

This sense of the future is important to bear in mind as one
thinks of ongoing controversies among Christians on the
qualifications for priesthood. As T.F. Torrance observed many
years ago, church worship must have a future dimension and
reflect world-wide perspectives.

Liturgy must allow the perfect pattern of the Kingdom of God to
do battle with the artificial patterns of our worship, in order that
through crucifixion with Christ they may be rent wide open, to
make room for the Advent presence of the Risen and Ascended
Lord (*Church Service Society Annual* of the Church of Scotland,
May 1954, pp. 17-18).

B.5. *Revelation 6.9-17; 7.1-4: Suffering and being Sealed*
For Christians the church in the world is not, and cannot be,
immune to the world's problems. If the world suffers, the
church suffers. The Christian communities may find themselves driven into a kind of ghetto by the world's persecution,
but this does not justify escapism and other-worldly retreat.
Some people assume (wrongly) that Revelation was produced
by an escapist sectarian group. Nothing could be further from
the truth. The book has a universal perspective and a sense of
world-wide mission and interaction with the world.

In sequence A.4. we have seen how the Lamb of God was
found worthy to open the sealed document (5.5). As the seals
are opened the four horsemen appear, symbols of death and
destruction, warfare, famine and pestilence (see sequence
D.1.). The cities of Asia Minor suffered severely in the first
century from such destructive forces, and also from major
earthquakes (the sixth seal—6.12). The Christians suffered
with their communities; in addition they suffered as they were
singled out, treated as scapegoats and persecuted (just as the
Emperor Nero selected the Christians and blamed them for
the fire in Rome). These are the souls beneath the altar
'slaughtered for the word of God and for the testimony they
had given' (6.9). Not surprisingly, they cry out with the
urgency of those who have suffered enough, who feel that the
world cannot endure much more, and who themselves are
waiting, like 'midnight's children', for their new birth.

God's punishment of evildoers, traditionally conceived in
Old Testament terms as the day of God's wrath, comes from
the four corners of the earth and will affect all creation pro-
gressively. The suggested fractions are a tenth, a quarter and
a third. In no way are the Christians spared from earthquake
and plague, but they are sealed by God so that they may witness effectively. Remember that the seals on the document are
the guarantees of the witnesses; so the seal on the forehead is
a guarantee of witness! And the number of those sealed
(144,000) is not the maximum number of the elect. Like Israel
in the Old Testament it is a representative sign to the nations
(Isa. 49.6), a symbolic number in relation to the infinite
possibilities of universal mission.

Adela Y. Collins has written about the significance of holy war traditions in Revelation. The present scenario is one of passive resistance, rather than the violent revolution attempted by the Zealots. But it is important to notice that the role of the elect, those who are sealed to be the 'first-fruits', is not entirely passive. They do not merely wait around for someone else's victory.

> The elect are not purely passive because the deaths suffered by members of the community are thought to play a role in bringing about the turning point, the eschatological battle... The faithful are to suffer persecution and death in the present. They expect a violent resolution of the conflict in which heavenly forces will defeat their adversaries. Their contribution to this outcome may be made in the form of a martyr's death, which hastens the end, because a fixed number of martyrs must die before the eschatological battle (*JBL* 96/2, 1977, pp. 255-56).

B.6. *Revelation 11.1-3: The Two Witnesses*

The two witnesses are symbols of the mission of the church in these difficult days. There is an attractive and, I think, compelling interpretation that identifies these witnesses with the saints Peter and Paul, both of whom, according to tradition, met their deaths in Rome during the Emperor Nero's persecution. Paul was beheaded and Peter was crucified. Clement of Rome describes both apostles as leading examples of those who 'contended to the point of death' (The sporting imagery is Paul's own in 1 Cor. 9.24-27). The Roman historian Tacitus sets the scene for this general persecution of Christians (*Annals* 15.44):

> Mockery of every sort was added to their deaths. Covered with the skins of beasts, they were torn by dogs and perished, or were nailed to crosses, or were doomed to the flames and burnt, to serve as a nightly illumination when daylight had expired. Nero offered his gardens for the spectacle.

Peter and Paul, as depicted in the Acts of the Apostles, are both the pioneers and major representatives of the church's mission. Luke sees their work as parallel and symbolic. Paul himself explains, in Gal. 2.7-8, how it could be said that Peter and Paul had divided the world between them in God's service:

I had been entrusted with the gospel for the uncircumcised, just as Peter had been entrusted with the gospel for the circumcised (for he who worked through Peter making him an apostle to the circumcised also worked through me in sending me to the Gentiles).

The critical period of activity of the two witnesses is the same duration as the trampling of the holy city. Forty-two months, or one thousand two hundred and sixty days, is three and a half years, which is the duration of crisis in the traditional calculations of time in apocalyptic vision (see Dan. 7.25). But it is also the time-span of the Jewish War and the siege of Jerusalem (from Spring 67 until 29 August 70 CE), the dramatic sequel to Nero's persecution. While apocalyptic prophecies conventionally work by modifying traditional symbols, it may not be a superficial coincidence if they can point to particular events with uncanny precision. We are dealing with a theological reinterpretation of a sequence of momentous events, rather than simply the prediction of the world's end, which may well prove to be mistaken.

B.7. *Revelation 11.4-13: Olive Trees and Lampstands*
As a result of the experience of the church in Nero's day, and in the following years, the ideas contained in the word 'witness' must include the readiness to die for one's faith. Witness means facing up to death. It is not only evidence that one possesses and hangs on to; it is also something that a believer is prepared to communicate to others in the spirit of prophecy, and it is something for which one is ready to give up all, in the surrender of life itself.

Witness is a prophetic activity, consistent with the tradition of Old Testament prophecy. The Christian experience of hardship and rejection is strictly comparable with Elijah's. Those who rejoice at the death of the witnesses do so 'because these two prophets had been a torment to the inhabitants of the earth' (11.10). The reasons and reactions are the same as those which greeted the prophetic troublers of Israel (see 1 Kgs 18.17). And the prophetic activity is authoritative, powerful in a way that compares with that of Moses and Elijah (11.5-6). And it is a preaching of repentance, because the sackcloth the prophets wear (11.3) is a symbol to encourage penitence. The witnesses are also identified with the esoteric imagery of Zech. 4.1-14. This means that they see things God's way. They share his universal perspective as 'eyes of the Lord which range through the whole earth' (seven lamps on a lampstand) and are anointed agents of God's purpose (two olive trees). For the Seer, Christian witness follows the path of Christ from suffering to glory. In their deaths the martyrs are symbolically associated with Christ's crucifixion (11.8). Like Christ also they have their Easter Day (11.11) and their day of ascension (11.12). God's kingdom is universal, but works through human agencies and representatives such as these. It is a situation of cosmic confrontation, because the powers of evil ranged against God's purpose for the world are no mere phantoms. The prophetic figure presents the gospel to the world and offers the occasion for repentance. The prophet may be an isolated individual or representative of the church, but as witness he or she speaks with God-given authority, accompanied by actions which are a powerful symbol and testimony.

Summary of Section B:
Visions of the Church in the World

Let anyone who has an ear listen to what the Spirit is saying to the churches

This expression is repeated in all seven of the letters to John's churches in Asia Minor. It is rarely studied because it is assumed to be a catchphrase associated with these coded secret messages. But the reverse is the case, as Anne-Marit Enroth demonstrates (in *NTS* 36/4, 1990, pp. 598-608):

The Hearing Formula is an invitation and an encouragement to hear. It underlines what should be heard and how it should be heard, and what follows from hearing aright...It is openly directed towards the communities mentioned in the letters, who in fact represent the whole church...The Hearing Formula is positive, for it does not contain the idea of judgement or of hardening. On the contrary, it underlines the promise and possibility of salvation.

Every aspect of these extracts which describe the church—worship and witness, being Christ-centred and coping with fierce opposition, showing a spiritual effectiveness, working out one's ministry in terms of priesthood and prophecy—is capable of a direct translation into the situation of today's church in the modern world. Revelation offers significant and positive ideas for those with ears to hear. On these grounds the beleaguered apocalyptic community cannot be dismissed as an outdated, self-conscious irrelevance.

If anyone had been tempted to think differently, a visit to Canterbury Cathedral on the morning of Sunday 9th December 1984 would have put them right. There is the site of Thomas à Becket's martyrdom, there is the chapel of the Modern (twentieth century) Martyrs, and there in the pulpit was Bishop (now Archbishop) Desmond Tutu, preaching a most impressive sermon about the power of God expressed through the witness of individual Christians, and proclaiming his Christian confidence in words from Revelation 7.9-12:

> After this I looked and there was a great multitude that no one could count, from every nation, from all tribes and peoples and languages, standing before the throne and before the Lamb, robed in white, with palm branches in their hands. They cried out in a loud voice, saying, 'Salvation belongs to our God who is seated on the throne, and to the Lamb!...Amen! Blessing and glory and wisdom and thanksgiving and honor and power and might be to our God forever and ever! Amen.'

(See further on this text section 2 in sequence E: Visions of the Future)

C. Visions of Creation

C.1. *Revelation 4.8-11: Hymn of Praise to the Creator*
In sequence B we were reflecting upon the experiences of the Christian community in the social world in which it lives. But what of the physical world, the natural environment for all human beings? did John's religious community have views about that, which might be mirrored in his visions?

The Judaeo-Christian tradition has been fairly consistent in affirming a view of the world as created by the activity and

command of God; at least this is the teaching in the account of
the seven days of Creation in Gen. 1.1–2.4 which is a primary
reference point in the biblical tradition. The world is God's
world and fundamentally good. Such a positive view of
Creation is affirmed in the Apocalypse by the twenty-four
elders (representative figures of the heavenly council) in a
song of praise: 'you created all things, and by your will they
existed and were created' (4.11). It is reasonable to assume
that the hymn would be echoed by every creature (as in 5.13),
and more particularly by John's church at worship 'on the
Lord's day' (1.10).

Such harmony cannot be quite complete. Creation is good,
but what of the matter from which it is created? The doctrine
of 'Creation from Nothing' was an attempt to avoid the dualism
between good creation and evil matter which preoccupied
Gnostics and Manichees. Dualism was there in the Babylonian
account of creation from which the writers of Genesis
borrowed; the god Marduk brought order out of chaos, but
the battle had to be renewed each year as the rivers of
Mesopotamia overflowed. The biblical writers were more
confident of God the Creator's omnipotence. But in Revelation
the hymn to the Creator follows the Trisagion (4.8); the
reaffirmed holiness of God cannot ultimately tolerate the presence of evil (see Isa. 6.5-7). Some aspects of the good Creation
have become corrupted and must be reformed or purged. But
for the moment the seer is content to be enveloped in the
heavenly liturgy.

A poem by R.S. Thomas, entitled 'Alive', offers a modern
statement of this positive theology of creation:

> It is alive. It is you, God. Looking out I
> can see no death. The earth moves, the
> sea moves, the wind goes on its exuberant
> journeys. Many creatures reflect you, the flowers
> your colour, the tides the precision of your
> calculations. There is nothing too ample,
> for you to overflow, nothing so small that your
> workmanship is not revealed. I listen
> and it is you speaking. I find the place where you lay

warm. At night, if I waken, there are the sleepless
conurbations of the stars. The darkness
is the deepening shadow of your presence; the silence a
process in the metabolism of the being of love.

C.2. *Revelation 6.12-17: The Great Earthquake*

We have already paused at these verses (in sequence B.5).
Then the emphasis was on the 'sealing'—the protective care of
God for his saints and martyrs; now we turn to the event that
follows the opening of the sixth seal, when all—especially 'the
rich and powerful' (6.15)—cower before what they interpret as
the judgment of God. What is happening here? Is it a natural
disaster, as when Mount Etna erupts and a productive area of
Sicily is buried beneath a lava flow? Is it what insurance
assessors call an 'act of God', when there is nobody else to
blame?

Several of John's seven cities had recent direct experience of
destruction by earthquake (e.g. Sardis, Philadelphia and
Laodicea). This region was particularly vulnerable to tremors,
as parts of Turkey are today. John can relate to this direct
experience and further intensify it, using traditional symbolism, to make of it a solemn warning, an anticipatory 'sign
of the end'. The world is destined to experience a catastrophe,
magnified many times beyond recent 'acts of God'. John uses
most immediately the apocalyptic material from Mk 13.8/Lk.
21.11 (several earthquakes become a 'great' one) and Lk. 23.30
('say to the mountains, "Fall on us"'). Already the 'larger than
life' or cosmic dimension is apparent in an event that affects
'every mountain and island' (6.14) as well as sun, moon and
stars (6.12-13). The further ingredients are derived from
several descriptions in the Old Testament of the ultimate Day
of Yahweh: the blood-red moon from Joel 2.31; the rolling up
of the sky like a scroll from Isa. 34.4; from Hos. 10.8 the destruction of Samaria which provokes a call for the mountains
to cover the shame; and the question 'Who is able to stand?'
from Mal. 3.2.

This extract offers a first, admonitory glimpse of that nightmare scenario—the natural world dislocated and crashing to
its doom. Perhaps the most terrifying aspect is that it occurs in
the midst of present social and political realities (the facts of

the first century CE Roman Empire as depicted by the four horsemen—see sequence D.1 below). Artists have often striven to depict such a nightmare. In the aftermath of the Napoleonic Wars Francis Danby (1793–1861) painted in the grand apocalyptic manner. His picture 'The Deluge' hangs in the Tate Gallery. Ten years previously in 1828 he had painted 'An Attempt to Illustrate the Opening of the Sixth Seal'. A comparable symbol, but much less realistic in manner, is Vincent van Gogh's 'The Starry Night' painted at the asylum at Saint-Remy in June 1889 and described as 'a lyrical delirium without precedent'. Philip Callow writes:

> High over the sleeping town of Saint-Remy, birthplace of Nostradamus, nocturnal prophecies stream through the firmament... Flame-like cypresses thrust the eye upward. The whole sky sizzling with volts is a great field, a playground, the land beneath it reduced and subjected. Here is the grand attempt to merge night and day, to combine sun and orange moon in one glittering vastness. Below the writhing of 11 exploded stars creep the stiff lines and angles of a town busily complete in itself and insulated against revelations, with a thin church spire looking strangely northern as it pokes up to prick the horizon (*Vincent van Gogh: A Life*, Allison & Busby, 1991).

C.3. *Revelation 8.6-13: Ecological Crisis*
The apocalyptic narrative gathers momentum as we move from the seven seals to the seven trumpets. The sixth seal, indeed, has given advance warning of the nightmare scenario, but the other seals are concerned with present realities. It is bad enough that Death already affects 'a fourth of the earth, to kill with sword, famine and pestilence, and by the wild animals of the earth' (6.8); but the target of the new sequence of trumpets is a third, not a quarter. The consequences of the first four trumpet blasts attack the earth, salt and fresh water, heavenly bodies and the atmosphere. At this stage the 'Green' reading of Revelation, with its projections of environmental disasters, sounds very compelling. What Jurgen Moltmann (*God in Creation*, London 1985, p. xi) called 'a life and death struggle for creation on this earth' has begun.

The ecological crisis is shown in pollutions of air, earth and water as well as in the over-use or misuse of finite natural resources. As Jonathan Clatworthy writes, western society in particular seems convinced

> that all natural phenomena (i.e. those not produced by human interference) are undeveloped and therefore valueless. Mountains of ice in Antarctica, Brazilian rain forests and the bottoms of oceans, while undeveloped, do not contribute to any economic activity and are therefore of no value until they are brought within the orbit of human development (*Theology in Green* 2, 1992, p. 8).

What is needed is a world-view that challenges both the basic concept of economic development, with its associated value-systems, and the reading of Gen. 1.28 to which it might appeal as a proof-text.

> According to the Bible, man's lordship over the world is justified because he is made in the image of God. According to Bacon and Descartes, it is man's rule over the world that substantiates his divinity (Jürgen Moltmann, *The Future of Creation*, London 1979, p. 128).

An 'environmentally-friendly' interpretation of the extract from Revelation would show how the earth, seas and rivers, the ozone layer and the solar system have all been polluted and seriously damaged by human ambition and greed. To replace a pervasive economic system with a 'Green Theology', that is, to respect God's role and purpose in the universe he created, and to value natural creation as good, appears to be a way of heeding the angels' trumpets before it is too late. That it is an issue for scientists as well as the religious community is shown by the 1990 appeal, *Preserving and Cherishing the Earth* (see *Christianity and Crisis* 14, May 1990), which notes that we

> are now threatened by self-inflicted, swiftly moving environmental alterations about whose long-term biological and ecological consequences we are still painfully ignorant... Mindful of our common responsibility, we scientists urgently appeal to the world religious community to commit itself, in word and deed, and as boldly as is required, to preserve the environment of the Earth. As scientists, many of us have had profound experiences of awe and reverence before the universe. We understand that

what is regarded as sacred is more likely to be treated with care and respect. Our planetary home should be so regarded. Efforts to safeguard and cherish the environment need to be infused with a vision of the sacred.

C.4. *Revelation* 10.1-11: *No Further Delay!*

Again, it is clear that time has moved on in the seer's narrative. While the opening of the sixth seal revealed a nightmare-vision which anticipated the end of the world (6.12-17, see C.2. above), and the fifth seal produced the imploring cry from the martyr-souls, 'How long will it be before you judge and avenge our blood?' (6.10, see B.5. above), now the critical period has arrived and 'there will be no more delay' (10.6). The 'mighty angel' who confirms this with an oath (10.5) is a direct messenger from God, a cosmic figure who wears about him fourfold signs of God's presence in the universe (cloud, rainbow, sun and fire—10.1). So he swears by God as Creator (10.6) that the schedule of God's plan is now to be implemented. John found the prototype of this angelic figure in 'the man clothed in linen' who, when asked 'How long?' swears in a similar oath that 'it would be for a time, two times and half a time' (Dan. 12.6-7). As it is revealed to John, this same apocalyptic time-scale of $3\frac{1}{2}$ years (or its equivalent in months or days) is about to start (11.2-3).

Thus the period of the last days is implemented, without further delay. As G.B. Caird argued, the message from a further sequence of seven, 'the seven thunders', is not recorded (10.4); the sealing-up amounts to suppression rather than the traditional idea of preservation for a later date (compare Dan. 12.9). So God short-circuits further delay; in mercy

> God has cancelled the doom of which they [the thunders] were the symbol... John is told to break in upon the sordid cavalcade of human sin and its ineluctable nemesis, because this is precisely what God himself has done. Humanity must be stopped forthwith from endlessly producing the means of its own torment and destruction. 'If the Lord had not cut short the time, not a living creature could have escaped' (Mark xiii. 20) (*The Revelation of St. John*, London 1966, pp. 126-27).

John's communication from the mighty angel is a sworn declaration about the 'mystery of God' (10.7), or the plans of God, previously prophesied but until now shrouded in mystery. The communication is also symbolized by the 'little scroll' (10.9) which the Christian prophet duly receives and absorbs. The bitter/sweet scroll is a vivid and accurate image for the nature of the prophetic experience—a glorious vocation from God which must be agony to pursue ('it will turn your stomach sour', NEB). It is not just a matter of prophesying blessing for the faithful and a curse for the faithless. Certainly this traumatic yet transcendent destiny was the regular experience of the Old Testament prophets. The prototype for John's scroll is to be found in Ezek. 2.8–3.3. Rev. 10.11 indicates not only the wide application of the seer's message, but also the compulsion that a prophet feels to discharge the commission God has given. As Amos 3.8 expressed the idea proverbially, 'the lion has roared; who will not fear? the Lord God has spoken; who can but prophesy?' The actual content of the scroll, which made John's stomach bitter, is the subject matter of ch. 11 (see sequence B.6 and 7 above).

C.5. Revelation 11.15-19: The Kingdom of God
In the 'apocalyptic' chapter of Luke's Gospel (Lk. 21, compare Mk 13), it is said:

> There will be signs in the sun, the moon, and the stars, and on the earth distress among nations confused by the roaring of the sea and the waves. People will faint from fear and foreboding of what is coming upon the world, for the powers of the heavens will be shaken... Look at the fig tree [see Rev. 6.13] and all the trees; as soon as they sprout leaves you can see for yourselves and know that summer is already near. *So also, when you see these things taking place, you know that the kingdom of God is near* (21.25-26, 29-31).

Luke uses a description of turmoil in nature in much the same way as John does for his nightmare scenario following the opening of the sixth seal (see C.2. above). Luke's 'unnatural' imagery is associated in some way with the historical event of the fall of Jerusalem at the end of the Jewish War (Lk. 21.20). This hardly appears to be the most auspicious moment to look for the realization of God's kingdom. In Revelation 11, John has been describing the fate of the 'two witnesses', probably the historical events of the martyrdoms of Peter and Paul in

Rome. Because these martyrs are united with their Lord in death, resurrection and ascension, Rome is merged symbolically with Jerusalem (11.8). The moment of martyrdom (and consequent setback for the church) again does not seem to be a good occasion for God's kingdom. But it is precisely at this moment that the dramatic juxtaposition is made, as the seventh—and last—trumpet sounds:

> The kingdom of the world has become the kingdom of our Lord
> and of his Messiah, and he will reign forever and ever...
> We give you thanks, Lord God Almighty...for you have taken
> your great power and begun to reign (11.15, 17).

Psychologically it could not be a better moment to realize the nearness of God's power. But it seems that John wants to say that the world is actually changing for the good, and not just that the reader's way of perceiving the world is changing and should change. The Old Testament tradition, especially in the Psalms, frequently speaks of the reality of God's kingly power and of the decisive moment of God's enthronement in Jerusalem (Mount Zion), perhaps through the coronation of an earthly monarch as God's agent (messiah). Psalm 2 is a good example of these ideas, not least because of the way it is applied by John in ch. 11 and elsewhere (see 2.27; compare Acts 4.25-26). When human rebellion against God has achieved its self-destructive worst—whether in political or in ecological terms—then God will seize power and reign. The underlying reality (that God is ultimately in control) will become a total reality, dramatically and explicitly revealed to all. An illustration from a modern hymn is apt here:

> 'The kingdom is upon you!'
> the voice of Jesus cries,
> fulfilling with its message
> the wisdom of the wise;
> it lightens with fresh insight
> the striving human mind,
> creating new dimensions
> of purpose for mankind.
> (Robert Willis)

Gustav Dalman wrote:

> There can be no doubt whatever that in the Old Testament and
> in Jewish literature the word *malkut* when applied to God always
> means 'kingly rule' and never means 'kingdom', as if to suggest
> the territory ruled by him (*The Words of Jesus*, Edinburgh 1902,
> p. 94).

This is a dangerous observation because it suggests that any
talk of God's lordship is only in terms of a spiritual abstrac-
tion. This is not true of Israel's religious nationalism (ultimately
a theocracy) in the Old Testament and is no more true of
those parts of the New Testament (e.g. Luke–Acts and
Revelation) where the kingdom of God must engage with
other political realities. Ultimately Revelation is saying that
the political dominance of Rome (with its religious, social and
economic implications) must yield to God's government, while
Luke–Acts declares that Christianity and Roman citizenship
are quite compatible.

C.6. *Revelation 14.6-7, 14-20: The Harvest of the Earth*

For British readers 'harvest' may recall Harvest Festival, with
churches decorated with golden corn, fruit, hops and a harvest loaf. But such a liturgical celebration of harvest can only
be traced back to Robert Stephen Hawker of Morwenstow in
North Cornwall, who on the first Sunday of October 1843
urged his parishioners to 'gather together in the chancel of
our church...and there receive, in the bread of the new corn,
that blessed sacrament which was ordained to strengthen and
refresh our souls'. In part this was a revival of the practice on
Lammas Day (1st August) in celebrations that were popular
in the Middle Ages. But the Harvest of the earth (both grain
and grape) in Revelation is something quite different.

In the Old Testament tradition both harvest and vintage
symbolize divine judgment, with the effect of purifying Israel
and eradicating its enemies. The closest parallel to Revelation
14 comes in Joel 3.9-17, where there is again a double harvest
of grain and grape. The context is that of the final battle and
of eschatological judgment, as all the nations gather outside
Jerusalem in 'the valley of Jehoshaphat'. In Joel 3.13 the
imagery corresponds exactly to Rev. 14.15, 18-19:

Put in the sickle, for the harvest is ripe.
Go in, tread, for the wine press is full.
The vats overflow, for their wickedness is great.

The winepress is a natural symbol for bloody vengeance, with
grape juice the colour of blood. The question for the reader is,
Whose blood?

R.H. Preston and R.T. Hanson pointed to a modern analogy
(in their Torch Commentary, London 1949, pp. 104-105):

We may be horrified at the picture of blood up to the horses'
bridles, but, after the experience of two world wars in one generation, many thinking people are much more ready to admit that
the root cause behind this terrible effusion of blood is not
ignorance, or social conditions, but sin, the breaking of God's
fundamental laws. They have seen in the history of the last
twenty-five years the wine-press of the wrath of God.

But should not we recoil not only at the scale of the slaughter
but also at the idea of slaughter as punishment by a just (and
loving?) God? The rider on the white horse in Revelation 19
(see sequence A, above) is a figure of the last judgement; 'he
will tread the winepress of the fury of the wrath of God the
Almighty' (19.15). His robe is bloodstained; but is this like
Isa. 63.1-2, or does John intend it to be the blood of his own
self-sacrifice?

'The wine press was trodden *outside the city*' (14.20). This is
associated both with the place of crucifixion and with the
theology of the writer to the Hebrews: 'Jesus also suffered
outside the city gate in order to sanctify the people by his own
blood. Let us then go to him outside the camp and bear the
abuse he endured' (13.12-13). Reference could then be made
to the martyrdom of the saints, as the 'first fruits' described in
14.4. Certainly harvest and vintage stand together as parallel
symbols in the structure of ch. 14. The context is the ultimate
judgment of the earth which is now ordered. The analogy is
the natural—and liturgical—process which begins with the
offering of the first fruits (Exod. 22.29), continues with the
grain harvest of Pentecost (Weeks), and ends with the grape
harvest at Tabernacles. It is important to remember that
harvest in Revelation has at least as much to do with rescuing
and preserving the crop as with destroying the rampant

weeds. The model is then the gospel parable of the weeds (Mt. 13.24-30, 36-43).

C.7. *Revelation 18.21-24: The End of the Known World*
The quartet by Olivier Messiaen, *Quatuor pour la fin du temps,* is known to have been inspired by John's apocalyptic vision of the end of the world. The music was written for fellow captives, after France had fallen and while the composer was a prisoner of war. The first performance took place in 1941 in Stalag VIIIA, Silesia, before an audience of 5000. A string on the cello was missing and the piano keys stuck. But the work remains one of the most horrifying and desolate in the repertory of chamber music. There is mystery, despair and agony in the long-drawn-out solos of the clarinet in the third movement and of the cello in the fifth; there is bitter stridency in the angular rhythms and melodies, deathly colours and sublime resignation. It is a lament for the loss not only of civilization but of life itself.

The destruction of Babylon was announced by the second flying angel:

> Fallen, fallen is Babylon the great! She has made all nations drink of the wine of the wrath of her fornication. (14.8)

The theme is developed throughout ch. 18 with authoritative utterance and symbolic action from angels and heavenly voices, and in between come the laments of kings, merchants and shipmasters. The issue is the predicted end of a political, social and economic system which seems to span the known world—the end of the Roman Empire and all that it represents. This momentous event is what Thomas R. Edgar calls

> the destruction of a system of international economic or commercial interests that has its headquarters in a major city. This economic entity has exercised influence or control over all the political rulers and governments of the earth (*JETS* 25/3, 1982, p. 341).

The analogy could be with the sudden end of the British Raj in India, the termination of any colonialist power, the end of Communism and the USSR, or the collapse of United States hegemony.

Karl Marx was attracted to use the imagery of the beasts in Revelation to convey the realities of historical capitalism. Recently the theory of the World System, propounded by Immanuel Wallerstein in 1974, to the effect that historical capitalism is the unifying process of world history, has been related to this apocalyptic paradigm by Kenneth Durkin, in an unpublished article:

> It is a social system in which those who operate by its rules have such a great impact that they create the conditions which force others to conform to the patterns or suffer the consequences [see Rev.13.16-17]... The world-system of historical capitalism is the shape of the one social system which has evolved in order to transform the natural world into utilizable form. Unfortunately it is a system where part of the process, the accumulation of capital, has become the ultimate objective of the system, utilizing the human social capacity to transform the world for this end.

Whichever system (e.g. the ancient Roman Empire or historical capitalism) one prefers to see as the subject of the lamentations and divine judgment of Revelation 18, this imagery emphasizes both the human pretentions and the ultimate fragility of the system. Human beings and divine creation are exploited in ways that are contrary to the ultimate purpose of the Creator. God's judgment is decisive and comprehensive. For us who are within the system it is the end of the world as we know it.

Summary of Section C: Visions of Creation

For the present, the glorious celebration of the world around us and of its Creator has given way to a scenario of nightmare, a realization of the extent of the ecological crisis, and a sense of the fragility of an apparently self-sufficient social and economic system. The time of God's harvest is at hand, when he will call all producers to account, and rescue the good produce from the weeds. Harvest is a time of judgment; it is also a time for triumphant celebration, as the God of Creation is enthroned in glory and the reality of his ultimate power is fully acknowledged. For the Christian community which suffers in the world—and cares desperately for the redemption of the world—John's message is that the fear and foreboding are held in tension with the hope and joy expressed in the anticipatory hymns of heaven. Here on earth there are still other powers with which the church must reckon, powers that rival God and seem set to destroy, with their self-destructive impulses, not only goodness but the whole creation.

D. Visions of Rival Powers

D.1. *Revelation 6.1-8: The Four Horsemen of the Apocalypse*

Rex Ingram made the silent epic *The Four Horsemen of the Apocalypse* for screening in 1921; it is often regarded as the first 'modern' film because of its techniques in cutting and production. In a memorable scene, Rudolph Valentino as a French soldier is on night reconnaissance during World War I, moving stealthily through the downpour. A German officer, who happens to be his cousin, creeps towards him. They meet in no-man's land, recognizing each other by the light of a starshell. A moment later they are engulfed in a massive explosion. The battle scenes are amazing, as are the sight of the four supernatural figures of horsemen riding out of the storm clouds, and a sea of crosses covering the landscape at the end. The film is based on a Spanish novel indicting German behaviour in the war and trying to persuade Spain to join the Allied side. There are no sympathetic Germans in a typical film which 'hates the hun'.

Similarly it was a 'world at war' about which the author of Revelation wrote, for the benefit of his Christian communities. It was equally vital for him to differentiate sharply between the 'good' and the 'bad' in his story. But the contrasts could be even more effective on occasion by means of parody. We have seen this already in sequence A, at the point where John set up a superficial resemblance between the first of the four horsemen and the rider on the white horse in Revelation 19, in order that he might dramatize the differences. The image of the victorious warrior Christ succeeds, both by contrast with the Roman army's use of Mithras and in continuity with the Old Testament picture of the royal agent of Yahweh. The present sequence of 'Rival Powers' will be concerned with other contrasts of this kind, as the Seer identifies the evil forces who are in opposition to God in his world.

The four horsemen are best seen as caricatures, much as political factors and personalities might be depicted by a modern cartoonist. Traditional interpretation in the Ethiopian Orthodox Church has identified them as a collection chosen at random rather than a historical sequence of Roman emperors (1. Augustus–Tiberius–Constantine; 2. Vespasian–Titus; 3. Claudius; 4. Diocletian—also Mohammed!). In Europe in the late Middle Ages, faced with the need to explain great disasters such as the Black Death, the imagery of the four horsemen provided a personification of Death, merging with the activities of God himself, to be the ultimate cause of such events. But in the first century CE the horsemen are most likely to symbolize more 'down to earth' political factors in the Roman Empire (e.g. the cult of Mithras, international warfare, famine and plague). They are cast as parodies of the coloured horses to be found in Zech. 1.8-11 and 6.1-8, which symbolize God's control of 'all the earth'. But they have become caricature figures, heavy with symbolism; their functions are explained in three ways: by the colour of the horse, by the symbol (bow, sword, scales, name) that is carried, and by the interpretation of their activity. They appear as present realities, powers hostile to the earth, four of the first sequence of plagues. Although released as part of God's plan, the existence of such destructive forces must put God's ultimate control at risk.

The four horsemen represented menacing features in the contemporary political situation of the Roman Empire. For this reason, to interpret one of the horsemen now as Saddam Hussein of Iraq, as Philip Wilby did in his 1992 BBC video composition *The Cry of Iona*, would be entirely consistent with the original author's intention.

D.2. *Revelation 9.1-11: The Destroyer*
As the fifth trumpet is blown, the earth experiences the first of three 'events' called 'woes'. The sequences of numbers in the Apocalypse are complicated to understand, not least because they overlap. There are three explicit series of seven

plagues, heralded respectively by the opening of seals, the sounding of trumpets and the emptying of bowls. Even though some of the same symbols recur (particularly variations upon the Egyptian plagues of Exodus), commentators are by no means agreed that the second and third series are replays of the first. The plagues are directed at different recipients, and the scale of their effect is progressive. It is thus possible to trace through the series either a narrative moving to a climax, or a symbolic pattern reaching completion. A.M. Farrer drew attention in his commentary to the weighting given to the larger or smaller 'halves' of the series of seven (the four horsemen or the three woes). But the three 'woes' may also be a larger pattern (it extends beyond 11.14-15 and may encompass the sequence of bowls also). In origin 'woe' is simply an exclamation of despair (as 8.13) but it becomes the umbrella term for an apocalyptic sequence of disasters. H.B. Swete (Commentary, London 1906) made them into figures from Greek tragedy when he personalized them as avenging Furies. This would certainly suit the locust scorpions of the first 'woe'. But it is possible that such a larger pattern of three is derived from the traditional apocalyptic sequence of birth-pains, afflictions and the end (as described in Mk 13.7-23; 24-25, 26-27).

The 'star' (9.1) is a fallen angel, an evil power permitted by God to act. Stars are identified as angels in Revelation (see 1.20); but this Satanic figure should be contrasted with the angel 'from heaven' in 20.1 who imprisons the evil forces again in 'the bottomless pit'. This star may be the same as that called 'Wormwood' in 8.11 (see Jer. 9.15; 23.15 for the name). John has taken the myth of the fallen star (see Isa. 14.12-21) and combined it with features of a prophecy of Babylon's doom (Jer. 51) and an account of the Egyptian plague of locusts (Exod. 10.12-15) enriched by the prophetic interpretation of Joel. Thus the author of Revelation can describe the evil empire of Rome being destroyed (and destroying itself) in terms of the fate of both Egypt and Babylon.

The prophecy of Joel begins from a dramatic description of the natural disaster of a locust plague, like the devastation caused by a grassland fire (1.19). Within the book itself,

however, and even more in rabbinic interpretation, the locust
becomes a symbol first of invading armies (2.4-7) and then—
as composite creatures—of supernatural agencies of destruction at the end of time. What for Joel is a portent of the
eschatological Day of the Lord (2.30-31), God's army of judgment destroying until the people repent, becomes in
Revelation an interim stage towards the climax, a period of
'torture' strictly limited to 'five months' with a similar but vain
hope for repentance (9.20-21). Destruction is the name of the
exercise, and so the fallen angel is given such a name,
doubly-emphasized by being given in Hebrew and Greek.
'Abaddon' (Destruction) is a synonym for Sheol, the waiting-
room of death. 'Apollyon' (Destroyer) may refer to the Greek
god Apollo (certainly the Greek playwright Aeschylus suggested that Apollo meant—and therefore was—a destroyer)
and may even allude to the emperor Domitian's identification
of himself with Apollo.

D.3. *Revelation 12.18—13.8: The Beast from the Sea*
The beast arises from the sea as a direct response to the
satanic summons (12.18). This is in turn a consequence of the
dragon's fall from heaven (12.9—see E.3 and 4 below). So the
beast represents a wide-ranging power in this world and,
according to the Christian prophet, is motivated by Satan. To
discover more, we need to investigate the background to
Revelation's imagery. The Old Testament used such mythology to illustrate the belief that 'the dominant world powers
which threatened Israel and opposed God were reassertions of
the primeval chaos subdued at the Creation' (Kenneth Durkin
in an unpublished article). The seas (as the original waters of
chaos) had been put in their proper place at Creation (Gen.
1.9), but their assertiveness would need to be conquered
again—as in the crossing of the Red Sea at the Exodus (see
Isa. 51.9), so also in the last days (see Isa. 27.1). The work of
John Day (*God's Conflict with the Dragon and the Sea in the
Old Testament: Echoes of a Canaanite Myth*, Cambridge 1985)
should be consulted on the theme.

Revelation's beast combines most of the features from the
four beasts (world empires) of Daniel 7. John J. Collins (*The*

Apocalyptic Vision of the Book of Daniel, Missoula 1977, pp. 114-15) makes clear that we are dealing with potent symbolism and not just breaking a code:

> The four kings/kingdoms are presented in Daniel 7 as manifestations of the ancient chaos monster. It should be quite clear that we are not dealing here with a code which can be discarded when it is deciphered. We cannot say that the statement in Dan. 7.3 is adequately paraphrased in Dan. 7.17... The interpretation... is not intended to replace the vision or to provide an adequate substitute for it. It tells us only enough to make clear that Daniel was not witnessing a mythical drama unrelated to particular earthly events but an interpretation of contemporary history. That interpretation is provided by showing that the events in question conform to a mythic pattern.

In Revelation also the potency of the myth empowers the judgment against a contemporary reality of world politics. The beast expresses 'the magnitude and inter-relation of the developed human rebellion against God' (Kenneth Durkin). This rebellion is focused for the present in the international affairs of the Roman empire. Because in the first century CE no more comprehensive social system can be conceived than the Roman empire, the potential of political catastrophe for the world is maximized.

But it may well be that the empire contains a seed of its own destruction, or at least of its own mortality (13.3). The 'death-blow' which 'had been healed' is to the author's mind a blasphemous parody of the saving death of Christ ('a Lamb standing as if it had been slaughtered', Rev. 5.6). But, like other amazing things associated with the beast, the 'mortal wound' appears to enhance its authority. For those who know their mythology, however, this is a true sign of mortality/vulnerability, as in the judgment of God on the serpent and Eve in the garden of Eden (Gen. 3.15); like serpent/dragon (Rev. 12.9), like beast. According to the immediate application of this imagery, in the Roman empire there were widespread fears that the emperor Nero, though dead by his own hand, would return 'redivivus' at the head of troops from Parthia; this could be taken as striking evidence of Rome's blasphemous arrogance and ultimate fallibility. So the ten 'horns' of the beast (13.1) will eventually destroy 'Babylon' (17.16-

17). The seer believes that political forces within the Empire will undermine its economic, social and religious stability.

D.4. *Revelation 13.11-18: The Second Beast*

Third in the line of authority from the dragon—Satan in Revelation 12—and the Beast from the sea, comes the Beast from the earth. This hierarchy of authority appears as a grotesque parody of the sequence of communication in Rev. 1.1-2. From the point of view of the Beast from the sea, every successful public performer (like a comedian or magician) needs a straight man or an assistant. And the second beast (otherwise known as 'the false prophet', 16.13; 19.20) fills this role. Daniel supplies the prototypes, in the he-goat of ch. 8 and in the story of the statue in 3.1-7. But in the context of Revelation this beast, with Satanic powers of speech and magical skills, sustains the first beast in its parody of Christ the Lamb.

If the first beast represents the cult of the Emperor, with the full weight of Roman central authority, then the second beast stands for the personnel concerned with the cult at a local level. Earthly origins (13.11) point to the local setting; the second beast derives its authority from the first (13.12); and the second beast forces the population to make an image of the first beast and worship it (13.14-15). The Asiarchs (see also Acts 19.31) or members of the *koinon / commune*, or provincial council, could be charged with such responsibilities, and even function as priests of the imperial cult. They are less likely to have been professional magicians, to work the miraculous signs indicated in 13.13-15. This part of the description of the second beast remains problematic; it could be a mythological elaboration of Mk 13.22: 'false prophets will appear and produce signs and omens, to lead astray, if possible, the elect'. This was all part of the traditional expectations, fostered by apocalyptic writings (see also 2 Thess. 2.9-10).

There may have been corresponding realities, however, in the way the cult of the emperors was manipulated. Credulity and religious susceptibilities were exploited in a very eclectic system that made the most of local opportunities. Wonders were stage-managed, if not to the extent that Lucian

described when writing of Alexander of Abonuteichos in the
second century CE (*Alex* 12ff, 26). Suetonius tells how 'the
statue of Jupiter at Olympia which' the emperor Caligula 'had
ordered taken to pieces and moved to Rome, suddenly uttered
such a peal of laughter that the scaffolding collapsed and the
workmen took to their heels' (*Gaius* 57.1). Heron of
Alexandria describes the mechanics of a statue of Dionysus
which automatically squirts milk as well as pouring out wine
(*Druckwerke* 13.1). The sign of fire (13.13) is reminiscent of
Elijah (1 Kgs 18.38—see also Rev. 11.5); but in the different
context of the imperial cult it may refer to thunder and
lightning. In one of Martial's epigrams (9.86) the emperor
Domitian is called 'Thunderer of the Palatine' just as Jupiter
is the 'Thunderer of the Tarpeian'. Dio Cassius relates that
the emperor Caligula had a mechanical contrivance 'by which
he gave answering peals when it thundered and sent return
flashes when it lightened' (*Roman History* 59.28.6). Emperors
made effective use of quite advanced technology, as Suetonius
reveals in his description of Nero's Golden House (Domus
Aurea) with its revolving ceilings (*Nero* 31.2).

Much obsessive ingenuity has been spent on decoding the
'number of the Beast' (13.18) which the second beast applies
in a branding process. If 13 is a number of ill-omen, who
would work in room 666? More apposite could be the concern
about computerized banking and supermarket bar codes
involving 6-6-6 as a way of taking over the world! For it is
clear that 13.17 refers to some kind of economic sanction,
restricting trade.

As A.M. Farrer (p. 159) pointed out, the number 666 is
achieved mathematically by taking the square of 6 (=36) and
then triangulating it, that is, adding together all the numbers
up to and including 36. If the root number 6 is associated with
the mythology of Creation (that earlier proved so useful in
elucidating the imagery of the beast—see D.3), then the sixth
day is when humankind was created (Gen. 1.26-31). The
mathematics could then symbolize pushing human ambition
to its furthest limits—away from God. Certainly the 'week' of
Creation is widely influential in Revelation, with seven as
completeness and eight as 'the week + 1' (Resurrection on the

first day of the next week, or its blasphemous parody in Rev. 17.11, where the pretentious head really 'belongs to the seven').

Gematria is the calculation of totals from the numerical equivalents of the letters in a word; it sounds like a game, but it was played with great seriousness in the ancient world to tell fortunes or convey cryptic messages, usually in Hebrew or Greek. There is an alternative reading (616 for 666) in 13.18 which shows all the signs of making a text fit a desired solution—the name of the emperor Nero in Latin. In the context where the arrogance of Rome and the blasphemy of the Imperial Cult are condemned, several possible solutions of 666 are relevant: Nero's name in Hebrew, or the emperors Titus or Domitian in Greek.

D.5. *Revelation 16.12-16: Armageddon*

Hal Lindsay's *The Late Great Planet Earth* (Grand Rapids 1970) is one of the best-selling religious books of this century, with 28 million copies in print by 1990. It has been immensely influential in the Bible Belt and in the Christian political right of the United States of America. The book is a popularization of the apocalyptic passages in the widely used *Reference Bible* of C.I. Scofield. All the ancient prophecies are being fulfilled, so history must be moving to its climax. The Jews have come back to their Promised Land; soon the Temple will be rebuilt. When that happens the day of Armageddon is near and the world will plunge to ruin in nuclear and environmental catastophe. A terrible dictator (worse than Hitler, Stalin or Chairman Mao) will arise to be the Antichrist. (While Mikhail Gorbachev was in power—and his famous birth-mark could be seen as the mark of the Beast—it was a Soviet Antichrist. His departure caused the scenarios to be rewritten, and Saddam Hussein, the rebuilder of ancient Babylon—cf. Rev. 17, 18—became a candidate during the Gulf War). Most of the world will obey the Antichrist, and he will turn on the Jews; at the same time 144,000 Jews will convert to Christianity and start a crusade to evangelize the world. Then a decisive pitched battle will be fought with nuclear weapons in Palestine.

If Lindsay's scenario for Armageddon fails to convince as a modern application of the Apocalypse, it is still a fair question why this final battle (prepared for by the pouring of the sixth bowl's contents—16.12) should be associated with a place in Israel called Armageddon (16.16). The place-name 'in Hebrew' (strictly 'Har/magedon') would denote Mount Megiddo. But Megiddo is a city on the plain (see Zech. 12.11) not a mountain, and the range of hills, at least seven miles away, is usually called Carmel. Megiddo was, however, a famous battle-ground—the scene of a defeat of the Canaanites by Barak and Deborah (Judg. 5), and where King Josiah was defeated and met his death (2 Kgs 23.29-30; 2 Chron. 35.22-23). But how relevant are such significant but remote events of Old Testament history?

Perhaps we should ask why the place-name is given 'in Hebrew' when it would be just as intelligible as a Greek name from the Septuagint? An attractive explanation is that we have an approximation in Greek to the Hebrew term 'mount of assembly' which is used in Isa. 14.13. There it referred to the (mythological) mountain in the far north—'Zaphon'—on which the gods are believed to assemble, and which the presumptuous king of Babylon seeks to climb in blasphemous pride. This pagan tradition was adopted by the Hebrews in the poetry of Psalm 48.1-2: 'His holy mountain, beautiful in elevation, is the joy of all the earth, Mount Zion, in the far north, the city of the great King'. The ideal of all mountains (even including pagan hopes) is applied by the Psalmist to the actual Mount Zion on which the Temple stood. In this case Rev. 16.16 is saying that the final conflict will take place around Jerusalem (the 'mount of assembly'). The outcome is now predictable, because the battle-ground is chosen by God, who in the biblical tradition has already subsumed the power of all other citadels to himself. Can we say that the nature of the battle is more to do with the power-struggle between spiritual forces than with an actual conflict of World War III?

D.6. *Revelation 17.1-18: Babylon the Great*
Talk of a trade war between Europe and the United States of America hits the headlines. There is much emotive language about fair competition in the marketplace and the iniquities of tariff barriers for importers on the one side and of large government subsidies to producers on the other. Trade is the

lifeblood of world economies; it is what makes the world go round! But vital though this is, one should perhaps recall that the trade discussed is between developed nations, for the real benefit of the multi-national corporations. The countries of the Third World are helplessly manipulated; their prospects for life, and not only their economic development, are the real casualties of the monetarist system.

We have already seen (in C.7 and D.4, above) how the 'mark... of the beast' is concerned with economic sanctions and trade restrictions (13.17). Further, the lament over Babylon, which extends through ch. 18, has much to do with trade, and the grief of the merchants at Babylon's fall (18.11-19). So it is important that Babylon as a 'woman sitting on a scarlet beast' (17.3) should have an economic aspect to her interpretation. Analogies between ancient and modern theories of economics are precarious, but it is clear that the Roman empire opened up vast trading possibilities, and these contributed greatly to its well-being and stability. Imperial religion and the cult of Roma, the goddess of Rome linked with the imperial cult (and attested for at least five of the seven cities of Asia), would have both direct and indirect economic aspects. But some producers then (as now in the Third World) disadvantaged by shortages and trading restriction, would face crippling debt and commercial ruin. They would be justified in yearning for the demise of Rome, its blasphemous religion and its economic cartels.

As J.-P. Ruiz shows (*Ezekiel in the Apocalypse*, Frankfurt, 1989), Revelation used themes from Old Testament prophecy (Ezekiel as well as Daniel and Jeremiah) to denounce those hated features for which the Roman empire stands—an example unique to the New Testament of the classic oracle against a foreign nation. The Old Testament regularly used prostitution as a symbol for idolatry (sacral prostitution) and lack of faith in the true God (e.g. Jer. 2–3 and Hosea; see the ironic judgment in Isa. 23.17-18). On that basis it could then be applied more widely to include laxity in sexual morals and even commercial exploitation. John had earlier used the symbol with reference to the woman Jezebel and the trade-guilds of Thyatira (2.20-23); now he takes three motifs (the beast and the city of Babylon as well as the prostitute) from his prophetic sources and blends them into a metaphoric unity. In his vision this woman, animal and city must yield to another woman (the Church as the Bride of Christ) and another city (the New Jerusalem), through the agency of another animal (the Lamb that was slaughtered). In literary terms this is a splendid example of biblical intertextuality (interpretation within the Bible's own traditions). But it is clearly something else as well: an apocalyptic text which uses metaphors to confront real issues in a contemporary crisis.

D.7. *Revelation 20.1-10: The Millennium*

It is calculated that about 40% of the United States population are 'Born Again' Christians. Many may look for the end of the world in terms of a Rapture of the Saved 'to meet the Lord in the air' (1 Thess. 5.17) and a Millennium (to reign with Christ for a thousand years). There will be 'high management openings for can-do Christians'. Jesus 'needs saints who develop success patterns in this present real-life testing ground...Many leaders will be needed to reign over cities, nations, territories and millennium projects'. In this new era 'strikes by workers and oppression by employers will be unknown', and Jesus will be 'committed to the instant destruction of the insubordinate or rebellious'. 'He will not permit the practice or propagation of false religion in any form.' 'At the Last Judgment no oral evidence will be required as in human courts; from the recesses of the individual's own memory the whole story will be revealed and flashed instantaneously before His mind' (citations from Paul Boyer's *When Time Shall Be No More*, Harvard 1992).

Chapter 20 of Revelation is the biblical text that set the programme for a wide range of such literal expectations about the millennial kingdom, and the much larger sociological phenomenon of millenarian sects. Although a thousand years is undoubtedly a long time, it is conceived in the Apocalypse as only an interim during which Satan is imprisoned and those who share Christ's resurrection also fulfil a priestly ministry (20.6, see also 1.5-6; 5.9-10 in sequence B). The Millennium resembles an earthly triumph and vindication of the deaths of Christ and the martyrs. In the traditional doctrines of Roman Catholicism it has been regarded as an error to concentrate on the literal period of one thousand years for this earthly kingdom, rather than see it as a symbol for the prolonged but indefinite time of the Church (between the resurrection of Christ and the last judgment).

Two points are important: to keep the Millennium in proportion, as only a small part of Revelation's programme, and to study this section in the literary context of the book as a whole (see J. Webb Mealy, *After the Thousand Years*, Sheffield 1992). Apparent inconsistencies between the visions of the end have given literary critics opportunity for much speculative rearrangement. It is hardly surprising if historically there has been disagreement on the literal nature of the Millennium and on its relation to the second coming of Christ. For some who closely follow the actual order of Revelation the second coming (19.11-16) precedes the Millennium and these last events are established by divine cataclysm. For others who associate the second coming with the last judgment (20.11-15), the Millennium must come first; then the earthly reign of Christian saints is the climax, and yet the natural outcome, of a gradual but sustained activity of the church in the world. Both of these ways of interpreting Revelation have been widely influential through the Christian centuries. They may be labelled Pre-millennialist and Post-millennialist respectively, with reference to the timing of the second coming.

Essentially Christians have taken over the structure of the Jewish dream in Daniel 7, a dream of two ages (this age and the age to come) which fall either side of the coming of a son of man, and the saints' receiving the kingdom (Dan. 7.18). So the Millennium faces both ways: it is a divine vindication demonstrated on earth, and an earthly anticipation of heavenly conditions. In Daniel it would seem that the kingdom of the saints is God's final word, and not an interim event. But in Revelation God appears to be equally involved in the trial of humanity, the just sentencing, the new opportunity offered by resurrection for the Millennium, and the ultimate annihilation in 'the second death' of those rival powers opposed to God. In an exegetical 'tour de force' J. Webb Mealy combines the different and possibly inconsistent aspects of the text in a theological reflection upon resurrection and judgment. Modern sensitivities may take him further than Revelation:

> According to John, the millennium is the length of the just jail sentence that will be served by those who reject God in this life. And for him the last judgment is a picture of the gracious release granted to those who have served out that sentence... The negative mystery is that those who have rejected God's grace in their mortal lives will never allow themselves to be reconciled to him, even though in his mercy they are granted the gift of resurrection itself... The positive mystery is... that God's patience towards the human race, his grace, and his willingness to give opportunity for repentance never expire, come self-deception, come rebellion, come murder, come suicide. To the very end, and to the very final proof, enter them or not, the doors to his kingdom remain open (Rev. 21.25) (pp. 247-48).

E: Visions of the Future

E.1. *Revelation 3.7-13: Pillars in the Temple of God*
Revelation attaches particular significance to doors (cf. 4.1); they are what a modern idiom might call 'windows of opportunity'. The opportunity before the church at Philadelphia (its 'open door') was for outgoing missionary activity (cf. similar language used by Paul in 1 Cor. 16.9 and 2 Cor. 2.12). The city was well placed for communications with Phrygia, from its position on the route from Smyrna and Lydia. Ignatius later recognized this aspect, in his letter to the Philadelphians 9.1. But in John's message the church seems to be facing the prospect of disaster; the best that can be hoped for is survival and holding the ground. The real security then rests in a transcendent vision of 'the new Jerusalem that comes down from my God out of heaven' (3.12). With this major theme the sixth letter anticipates the climactic vision of John's book.

By association of ideas, talk of open doors leads to shutting and keys. The reference to 'the synagogue of Satan' (3.9) might allude to the shutting out of Christians, excommunicated by the Jews. But the conflict is more likely to be an internal Christian matter, similar to the issue with the Nicolaitans at Ephesus (2.6). Samuel Sandmel was equally

opposed to the theory of official Jewish excommunication and
suggested 'that the intent is to say that *true* Jews would not
oppose Christianity, and therefore those Jews who oppose it
are not true Jews' (*Anti-Semitism in the New Testament*,
Philadelphia 1978, p. 123). The struggling Christian community looks up to the authority of the key-holder who has
opened their door so that none can shut it (3.7). The risen
Christ is here depicted, in terms of the prophecy of Isa. 22.22,
as the prime minister, second only in authority to the king
himself in the Kingdom of God. Isaiah prophesied that
Eliakim would replace Shebna (22.15-19); his new authority
and duties are described (22.21-24); but 21.25 seems to
suggest an eventual removal from office. Isaiah's idea of 'a
peg in a secure place' becomes in Rev. 3.12 'a pillar in the
temple of my God'. Pillars remain standing when all else falls,
and so they are an image of stability in a volcanic region like
Philadelphia's, under constant threat of earthquake. These
are powerful metaphors of transcendence for a city that is
slow to recover and a church that looks disaster in the face.

The pillar is inscribed with the name of God and belongs to
the future city, the new Jerusalem (3.12). An inscribed 'new
name' is also found on a 'white stone' in the letter to
Pergamum (2.17). After recent archaeological excavations in
London have revealed burials with white pebbles in the
mouth, one might speculate that it was a concrete sign of a
Christian in the rite of passage to the future life. But in any
case Philadelphia is no stranger to new names; the city had
assumed new names as a vote of thanks to the Roman
emperor (under Tiberius it became Neocaesarea, and from
Vespasian to Domitian it bore the name Flavia Philadelphia).
Once again we read the signs of a power struggle between
Rome and the authority of Christ in the Kingdom of God.
Perhaps some enthusiasts in Philadelphia sought to anticipate
the new situation of the Kingdom. Colin J. Hemer has observed
that the later town (Alasehir) on the site of Philadelphia
makes a visual impact today that is strikingly 'foursquare'
(see 21.16); its groundplan reveals a 'square enclosure and
chess-board street pattern untypical of Turkish towns' (*Letters
to the Seven Churches*, p. 174). Possibly the local town was

trying to live up to the ideal of symmetry and make the promise its own, by converting it into an actual possession. Sir William Calder (*BJRL* 7, 1923, pp. 309-54) also believed that the prophetic movement of the heresy known as Montanism originated in the district of Philadelphia. Predictions of a physical descent of the new Jerusalem to earth were a vital part of Montanism, seeking to turn expectation into new reality.

E.2. *Revelation 7.9-17: Naught for your Comfort?*

> I tell you naught for your comfort,
> Yea, naught for your desire
> Save that the sky grows darker yet
> And the sea rises higher.

These words from G.K. Chesterton's poem 'Ballad of the White Horse' were used by Trevor Huddleston to focus attention on the plight of the non-Whites in South Africa as long ago as 1956. Alan Paton, another famous name from the same generation of the struggle in South Africa, wrote in his autobiography *Towards the Mountain* (New York 1980, p. 12) about

> the vision of John on Patmos, of that world where there shall be no more death, neither sorrow, nor crying, neither shall there be any more pain. The visions are ineffable, of a world that will never be seen, but towards which we journey nevertheless.

Huddleston sees the symbol of the storm clouds; Paton the power of an ideal, however unrealistic. In contrast Desmond Tutu seems to take the words of Revelation at their face value (see above, in the summary of sequence B). Like the author of Revelation himself, he acknowledges the spiritual encouragement achieved by combining the images of suffering and of hope. Again and again John speaks of the harshness of the world's sufferings and the heavenly peace of those who have overcome in the power of faith. It is no accident that the vision of 7.9-17 follows rapidly on the breaking open of the seals and the protective sealing of God's servants. In the same way the triumph and thanksgiving of 11.15-18 are the immediate

sequel to the account of the two representative witnesses in
11.3-13.

> True security will come when all of us, Black and White, know
> we count as of equal worth in the land of our birth, which we love
> with a passionate love. White South Africa, please know that...
> Blacks will be free whatever you do or don't do. That is not in
> question. Don't let the *when* and the *how* be in doubt. Don't delay
> our freedom, which is your freedom as well. Revelation 7.9-12 is
> the vision that upholds me. May it come true for our land
> (Desmond Tutu, *Hope and Suffering*, London 1984, pp. 101-102).

E.3. *Revelation 12.1-12: The Woman Clothed with the Sun*
Morris West's novel *The Clowns of God* (London 1981) takes
as its themes the world of apocalyptic and the ways that
church and society react to the idea of the second coming of
Christ. The novel is a compelling piece of storytelling with a
serious purpose. If you have read it, you will have your own
estimate of how satisfactory the conclusion is. If you have not,
I do not wish to spoil the ending for you, but perhaps I can
say that it has to do with a special celebration and recollection
of the birth of Christ, in unusual surroundings.

Chapter 12 of Revelation starts with a representation of the
birth of Christ. But the imagery and the theological emphases
are so different from the stories in Matthew and Luke that
you may not recognize it at first. The gospels lay stress on the
ministry and teaching of Jesus as well as his death and
resurrection. And the meaning of all these events in the whole
life was read back by Luke and Matthew and built into their
telling of the infancy stories as well. But Revelation starts by
depicting a woman in heavenly dress (Israel? Eve? Mary?)
and then moves rapidly from the birthpangs to the threatened
life of the child (the innocent who dies on the cross) and to the
purposes of God who takes Christ to himself (in resurrection
and ascension).

In Col. 2.14-15 Paul speaks of the consequences of Christ's
death on the cross and the cancellation of the bond of sin: 'he
set this aside, nailing it to the cross. He disarmed the rulers and
authorities and made a public example of them, triumphing
over them in it.' These same consequences are represented in
even more dramatic pictures in Revelation. There is civil war

in heaven between the hosts of angels, led by the archangel (and champion of Israel) Michael, and the powers of Satan. In Old Testament texts such as Job 1, Satan is a member of the heavenly council; but in subsequent Jewish and Christian interpretation he has changed roles from devil's advocate to devil. The heavenly triumph of Christ achieves a decisive realignment: the Satanic powers are expelled from heaven, for the earthly forces of the Christian church to contend with. The church's witnesses are well-equipped for the struggle. They are sustained by the victory that Christ has won (12.11) and the knowledge that God's consummation is near (12.12).

It has been argued forcibly by Adela Yarbro Collins (*The Combat Myth in the Book of Revelation*, Missoula 1976) that most of Revelation is influenced by a traditional structure known as combat myth, and this is seen especially clearly in 12.1-12. This typical pattern of combat derives from Near Eastern mythology, and it may be glimpsed in the Old Testament (e.g. Isa. 27.1; 51.9-10 and many Psalms). Essentially there are three phases: a rebellion of evil forces, often symbolized as monsters; the temporary dominance of the powers of chaos; and final victory for the forces of good. The contest, graphically described, is often linked to the ordering of creation, or to eschatological expectation. Revelation clearly uses such traditional resources of pictorial language, and the interrelation of suffering, punishment and victory is vital to the expression of the author's hopes. But John does not simply reproduce a standard pattern, either once or several times. And the narrative of ch. 12 is not complete at v. 12. The story goes on...

E.4. *Revelation 12.13-17: The Pursuit*
Of increasing importance in early Christian art is the representation of the mother of Christ, often central in the group of disciples and symbolic of the church as a whole. A good example is the picture of Pentecost in the Rabbula Gospels, a manuscript of the gospels produced in 586 CE in Eastern Syria. The twelve apostles are gathered with Mary, distinctively dressed in red-brown and black, in the centre of the picture. The Holy Spirit descends as a dove over Mary, and

there are tongues of fire above all thirteen figures.

In Revelation 12 the mother of Christ is pursued by the dragon, now that he is cast down to earth. She is preserved from this persecution (in circumstances that may allude to the flight of the Christians from Jerusalem to Pella at the time of the Jewish War). The dragon in his anger transfers the attack to the rest of the woman's offspring, that is the brothers and sisters of Christ, in the broadest sense of members of the Christian church.

This woman has a kaleidoscopic character in John's vision, embracing the sweep of salvation history, from the Old Testament to the current persecution of the Christians, from the daughter of Zion to the mother of believers. Even more significant is the deliberate contrast being made by John between this glorious figure and another woman, the person-ification of evil and blasphemy in the harlot of Revelation 17 (see D6 above in the sequence of Visions of Rival Powers). Again the author makes a deliberate association between the mother of Christ in Revelation 12 and the bride of Christ in Revelation 21.

There is another tradition in Christian art that makes out a major contrast between two women, the one blindfolded and carrying stone tablets who represents the Jewish Synagogue, and the other tall and graceful in power who is the Christian Church triumphant. We should observe that there is no basis whatsoever for this anti-Semitic contrast in Revelation 12. Rather John's kaleidoscope shows a continuity between Israel and the Church. This corresponds with the suggestion made above concerning 3.9 (see E.1.).

E.5. *Revelation 21.1-21: The New Jerusalem*
Until its demolition in 1961, there stood for three-quarters of a century at the top of Chatham Hill in Kent a massive building called Jezreel's Tower. It was not far short of a perfect cube with the dimension of one hundred and forty-four feet, built as an assembly room and headquarters for the Southcottian sect called the New and Latter House of Israel. In the long history of millennial movements and sects this is a striking example of trying to force God's hand by a literal implemen-

tation of prophecy. It is a fanatical attempt to build the new
Jerusalem on earth according to the blueprint of John's vision.
Of course the builders of the mediaeval cathedrals, like
Abbot Suger of St Denis, were also concerned to reflect the
symbolism of Revelation in their buildings. So there are twelve
bays with vaulting to represent the fact that the church of
God is built upon the twelve apostles. As we have noted
before, Revelation expresses in more visionary language truths
found elsewhere in the New Testament. So here Rev. 21.14
corresponds to the building metaphor in Eph. 2.19-22
where the apostles are the foundation and Christ himself is
corner-stone (or alternatively key-stone).

Just as the builders of the late mediaeval cathedrals created
a revolution in architectural terms, so John's vision of the new
Jerusalem has a major difference from any earlier visions of
heaven in Jewish apocalyptic. This holy city is seen in the act
of coming down from heaven (21.2). In this new creation the
gulf is bridged between earth and heaven. Jewish mystics and
Greek thinkers alike imagined correspondences between earth
and heaven. But on the basis of the gospel, Christians can
speak with confidence of the Incarnation and of God's
dwelling with his people in the transfigured conditions of this
world. Rev. 21.3 is possible because of Jn 1.14 and 3.13.

E.6. *Revelation 21.22—22.5: City and Garden*

A wealth of images are jostling for position in John's vision of
the new (or renewed) creation. There is the holy city and also
the paradise garden (as it was before the Fall). We should look
at each individual insight and resist the temptation to tidy it
all into a single landscape. The new city of Jerusalem is here
surveyed because of the symbolism of numbers and precious
stones, and even more because this measurement is the coun-
terpart of the measuring and the trampling of old Jerusalem
in the Jewish War (Rev. 11.1-2). The garden and the source of
water (so prominent in the van Eyck altarpiece mentioned
in the sequence A.4) themselves correspond to the imagery of
Gen. 2.9 and Ezek. 47.1.

'Those who conquer will inherit these things, and I will be
their God and they will be my children' (21.7). It is striking

that we find the heavenly city and paradise garden described
in terms that fulfil the promises made to those who conquer in
the seven cities of Asia Minor (Rev. 2, 3). The heavenly
Jerusalem, according to Colin J. Hemer (*Letters to the Seven
Churches*, p. 16),

> is set in implicit contrast with the imperfections of the seven
> actual earthly cities. The parallels are not... obtrusive or sys-
> tematic; there are repeated echoes of the same images,
> promises developed in a larger context, particular opponents
> overcome and disabilities reversed.

As we saw in sequence B.2, in the letter to Ephesus (Rev. 2.7)
the promise was made 'to eat from the tree of life, that is in
the paradise of God' (see 22.2). And the reference to God's
throne in the Laodicean letter (3.21) is resumed in 22.3. It was
to the church in Philadelphia that special mention was made
of 'the new Jerusalem that comes down from my God out of
heaven' (3.12, see E.1 above).

In John's vision the actual cities were scrutinized by the
risen Christ, and were to face a period of severe trial. We
observed in sequences A and B how features of the Son of
Man vision are made fundamental texts in all the messages to
the seven churches. Those messages also point forward, in a
less structured way, to the hope of New Jerusalem. Where
there is an inheritance promised to the victors in the church,
these promises are fulfilled in the climactic vision ('Those who
conquer will inherit these things', 21.7). The vision of hope
that is set before them could be understood in terms of spiritual development and blessing for the individual believer. But
it also clearly relates to an eschatological fulfilment and vindication that will be closely linked to the earthly facts of daily
life in the churches.

E.7. Revelation 22.6-21: The Risks of Prophecy

Revelation is a work of Christian prophecy, as this conclusion
makes clear. There is a general impression (not necessarily
historically accurate) that the voice of prophecy had been
silenced for centuries since the prophets of the Old Testament.
New religious movements, including Christianity, brought
an upsurge of prophetic activity in the first century, and a

recurrence of the practical problem: how do you test a prophet and know that he or she speaks the truth? The twentieth century experiences similar difficulties with the rise of charismatic movements in some churches.

The early Christians had their guidelines for testing prophets. Confidence tricksters were exposed by the amount of free board and lodging they claimed. There were also elements of a credal test of basic beliefs (how they measured up to the earliest gospel tradition, or the prototype creeds) in order to judge the truth of what they said. Immediate prophecy (22.10)—that is, not sealed up for the distant future, after the pattern of Dan. 12.9—could be vulnerable to corrupting interpretation and interpolation. A threat (22.18-19), which itself rests on the power of prophetic symbolism, might be adequate to discourage tampering.

John's is a burning personal faith that the Son of Man, whom he has glimpsed in glory, will be coming soon. For him Christ is the faithful and true witness who provides a direct link for the believer to the Father of all. The words of John's prophecy participate in this trustworthiness and truth (22.6). Like others in the early church (and in subsequent crises) he prays earnestly the Aramaic prayer 'Maranatha'—Come, Lord Jesus (22.20). Despite one's personal faith (or because of it) one yearns for the world to be confronted by the Risen Lord. In that way, perhaps, the unbelievers will be convinced and the souls of the believers and martyrs will be relieved from their duties of witness. Meanwhile the saints need the grace of Christ (22.21).

Summary of Section E: Visions of the Future

Samuel Wesley's well-known hymn 'Aurelia', with words by S.J. Stone, might be used to sum up Revelation's perspective of the Church, the promises made in the present and the vision of their future fulfilment:

> The Church's one foundation
> Is Jesus Christ her Lord...
> She waits the consummation
> Of peace for evermore;

Till with the vision glorious
Her longing eyes are blest,
And the great Church victorious
Shall be the Church at rest.

Some theological reflections by Jürgen Moltmann on 'The
Consummation of Creation', in which he applies texts from
Revelation 21, provide us with an underlying rationale for
visionary material of this kind:

> In the prophetic and apocalyptic visions we find two formal
> principles: first, the negation of the negative and, secondly, the
> [positive] fulfilment of anticipations. In this double form the
> visions remain both realistic and futuristic. The negation of
> what is negative—'death shall be no more, neither shall there be
> mourning nor crying nor pain any more' (Rev. 21.4)—defines the
> space that is open for the positive reality that is to come. The
> vision of 'the classless society' also follows this method of
> describing the future by means of a negation of the negative.
> But the mere negation of what is negative does not necessarily
> lead to a definition of the positive. Consequently eschatology too
> cannot be developed merely as negative theology...
>
> The victory of Christ over the forces of this world which are
> hostile to God would make it possible for Christians again to live
> in the cosmos, once more understood as creation. The expres-
> sions used to visualize the future and the new being of man do
> not go back to some presupposed primal condition; they explain
> the 'new thing' of the raising of the crucified Jesus by promising
> his lordship over everything, the dead and the living: 'The city
> has no need of sun or moon to shine upon it, for the glory of God
> is its light, and its lamp is the Lamb' (Rev. 21.23) (*The Future of
> Creation*, London 1979, pp. 124-25, 169).

Conclusions from These Five Sequences of Readings through Revelation

The five sequences have provided a schematic framework
within which we may organize blocks of material from
Revelation, in order to understand it better. We have seen
how certain fundamental statements were made about the
being of God, and the death and saving activity of Christ. The
primary context of the book, in which these theological claims
were made, was the present existence of a cluster of Christian

communities in Asia Minor, who were shown their responsibilities to bear witness to their faith and to die for it, if necessary. The larger context of thought was the whole world around them, which was in origin the good creation of God. But its future was threatened in terrifying ways. The positive side to this fear was the ultimate destruction of all those contrary forces and insidious movements of distortion which were dominating the world. John maintains that from the ashes of this destruction would come the restoration of creation as it should be, and the uniting of earth and heaven in the eternal worship of God.

However strange and multicoloured the language of Revelation may appear to be, it expresses a number of ideas very clearly:

1. The transcendent power of God as creator and of Christ as redeemer;
2. The relationship of believers through Christ to God in the Spirit;
3. The interaction of worship and witness for the church in the world;
4. The transitory nature of this age (even in its religious dimensions);
5. The element of self-sacrifice inherent in Christian witness;
6. The political implications of Christian living;
7. The power of a vision of hope in a context of suffering.

My thanks are due to the Bible Reading Fellowship for their kindness in allowing me to reuse and develop material from the Guidelines treatment of Revelation in this chapter.

3

WHAT KIND OF BOOK?
THE LITERARY CHARACTER
OF BOOK OF REVELATION

Is Revelation Distinctive?

SHOULD THE BOOK OF REVELATION be considered on its own, as a unique work? Some would maintain that Daniel in the Old Testament and Revelation in the New Testament stand alone as the only works of the literary type of 'apocalypse' in the biblical canon. But even this statement invites some form of comparison between them. It would be even more profitable to compare Revelation with other apocalyptic works, both Jewish and Christian, outside the limits of the Bible. There are approximately 15 Jewish apocalypses dating from the inter-testamental period and 24 early Christian examples. The comparison helps one to understand this type of writing, and the conventions associated with it—what the first readers of such a work would have taken as read.

> Generally speaking, apocalyptic is understood to mean a complex of writings and ideas which were widespread about the turn of the era in Palestine, in the Israelite diaspora and in early Christian circles; but which can also appear in similar form in other religious situations and mental climates...A second and narrower use of the word [is] the title of literary compositions which resemble the book of Revelation, i.e. secret divine disclosures about the end of the world and the heavenly state. The word apocalypse has become the usual term for this type of book. It is also applied to books and parts of books to which the ancient church did not as yet give this title—for example the synoptic apocalypse of Mark 13 (Klaus Koch, *The Rediscovery of Apocalyptic*, SCM Press, London 1972, pp. 13, 18).

Some Christian commentators have wanted to say that
Revelation is distinctive in early Christianity because it is a
prophetic rather than an apocalyptic book (cf. Chapter 2,
sequence E.7 above). It symbolizes the rebirth of prophecy in
the early Christian Church, after years in which Jewish
theology was seen in terms of Law rather than Prophecy, that
is, as scribal exposition focused on the Torah (the Pentateuch
or five books of the Law of Moses). Revelation as prophecy
should therefore be compared directly with the oracles of
Hebrew prophets contained in the books of the Old Testament
such as Isaiah, Jeremiah and especially Ezekiel, and the
scrolls of the Minor Prophets (particularly Joel, Zephaniah
and Zechariah).

But it is not easy to sustain the description of Revelation as
prophecy, if that is understood as a statement about literary
form (but also see below for observations about interpreting
tradition and on dramatic performance). The text does not
resemble consistently either the spoken or the subsequently
written (anthologized) oracles of the prophets. Revelation as
composition is a literary mixture of materials, only some of
which are oral in character: narratives of visionary experience,
letters, hymns, traditional mythology and bizarre imagery,
coded references to the sequence of historical events, stylized
threats of judgment and accompanying lamentations, symbols
of number and colour, projections of the future in terms of a
new (or renewed) order of creation. I suspect that Christian
writers describe Revelation as prophecy not because some of
its characteristic features are prophetic, but because they wish,
for apologetic purposes, to reclaim the work as Christian prophecy and, therefore, as inspired Christian preaching. But I
think we can appreciate the value of Revelation as a
Christian work within the context of the early Church
without misrepresenting its essential character in this way.

Definition of Apocalypse as a Literary Genre

What is the definition of the term 'apocalypse'? It denotes a
form or genre of literature. To say that the name derives from
a Greek word meaning 'that which is uncovered or revealed' is

only part of the definition, because that takes no account of the technical senses in which the Greek word is now used by scholars. As a modern term of classification of ancient literatures it does not include all ancient works that have 'apocalypse' in their title (e.g. *Apocalypse of Moses*), but it does include other texts or parts of texts that did not carry that label (e.g. *Testament of Abraham*).

We can trace the development of thought in the growing complexity of definitions of the genre 'apocalypse'. First comes Klaus Koch *Rediscovery of Apocalyptic*, justifying serious academic attention to the subject, in the words already quoted. Then we have John J. Collins on p. 9 of the introduction to *Semeia* 14 (1979), based on the constant elements in the paradigm established by the SBL project:

> 'Apocalypse' is a genre of revelatory literature with a narrative framework, in which a revelation is mediated by an otherworldly being to a human recipient, disclosing a transcendent reality which is both temporal, insofar as it envisages eschatological salvation, and spatial, insofar as it involves another, supernatural world.

Thirdly there is a three-fold definition by David E. Aune (*Semeia* 36, 1986 pp. 65-96) which incorporates both a critical appraisal of Collins' definition and some insights from David Hellholm and the International Colloquium on Apocalypticism at Uppsala in 1979:

> The definition should be formulated in terms of form, content and function... The proposed definition of the apocalyptic genre, with special reference to the Apocalypse of John, is as follows:
> 1) Form: an apocalypse is a prose narrative, in autobiographical form, of revelatory visions experienced by the author, so structured that the central revelatory message constitutes a literary climax, and framed by a narrative of the circumstances surrounding the revelatory experience(s).
> 2) Content: the communication of a transcendent, often eschatological, perspective on human experience.
> 3) Function: (a) to legitimate the transcendent authorization of the message, (b) by mediating a new actualization of the original revelatory experience through literary devices, structures and imagery, which function to 'conceal' the message which the text

'reveals', so that (c) the recipients of the message will be
encouraged to modify their cognitive and behavioral stance in
conformity with transcendent perspectives.

The Collins/SBL definition was subsequently expanded to
include some reference to function, in the light of comments
such as those of Aune and Hellholm. Collins had originally
classified the range of extant apocalypses under two main
types and further sub-categories. The Book of Revelation was
assigned to category Ib—Apocalypses with Cosmic and/or
Political Eschatology (which have neither historical review
nor otherworldly journey). This typology shows its subjective
aspect: not all scholars would agree that Revelation has no
review of history, even if its otherworldly journey is very limited in comparison with some apocalypses. There is real
danger in trying to build too much into an essentially generic
definition—the simpler it is, the more useful it can be. The
enlarged range of literary questions opened up by genre criticism are highly significant, but it may be better to treat them
under headings other than 'definition' later in this chapter.
Genre criticism is also important, perhaps more important, for
what it can reveal about divergency and variations, and not
just for classifying standard 'types'.

For practical purposes there is a range of questions that
need to be asked about the form, content and function of any
apocalypse:

Form	Who reveals?
	to whom?
	How (under what circumstances)?
Content	What is revealed?
	What is the declared purpose of the revelation?
Function	For what purpose is the literary text designed?
	Are there indications of early response to the text?

These are the aspects of the definitions of apocalyptic writing
that seem to me most important for Revelation. It is essentially
revelatory, and that revelation is made through a framework

of narrative. It is unlike the oracle of a prophet because the revelation comes through a mediator who is out of this world (the risen Christ or angelic figures) but who communicates directly to a human recipient (John). What is disclosed is transcendent, beyond this world; a kind of heavenly storeroom is opened up to John, the earthly visitor, so that he can see things which (although still in heaven) have a direct bearing on human affairs. The perspective is either a time sequence (such as linear history), so that at the appropriate moment these realities will appear on earth and so transform events as to bring about a final salvation. Or the perspective is of a spatial dimension concerned with the connection between worlds: the new vision is of a key relationship between local happenings and cosmic realities, so that the one is perceived through the other. Such visionary perspectives are born in a situation of crisis, so as to encourage or console the 'righteous' community in its sufferings. But an apocalypse is relevant not only to a time of crisis; in less stressful circumstances it goes on being used in other ways (e.g. to teach moral lessons by extreme example).

Additional Note on Apocalyptic and Apocalypticism

As we have seen already, 'apocalyptic' can be used strictly of the essential ideas of the literary genre, or (much more loosely) of a fashion of thinking and writing, characterized by a heightened sense of eschatology, or imminent expectation of the End-time. The problem of communication begins with this variability in the use of the word. It is possible to construct a synthesis, or identify a fairly coherent body of ancient thought, which starts from, but extends beyond, the literary apocalypses. But if one then relates this 'Apocalyptic', by comparative methods, to modern movements associated with political, social and environmental disaster, it is imperative to use strict criteria for this enlarged, comparative usage. Does the modern thinker, understandably scared of the nuclear holocaust, really express the same ideas in a similar context to John in the first century CE?

David Aune commends

> the three-fold distinction between 'apocalypses' (as literature),
> 'apocalyptic eschatology' (as a world view) and 'apocalypticism'
> (as a socio-religious movement) proposed recently by a number
> of scholars [as] an important step forward in the discussion... It
> can no longer be assumed that apocalypses were produced by
> apocalyptic groups who espoused a distinctive type of apoca-
> lyptic eschatology (*Semeia* 36, 1986, p. 67).

But it is probably safer to restrict the use of 'apocalyptic' to
denote the literary genre as the source of such ideas, and to
use terms like 'heightened eschatology' for looser references to
the ideas in general, and 'millennial' or 'millenarian' to refer
to the socio-religious movements.

We should try to safeguard 'apocalyptic' and 'apocalypticism'
as terms related to a literary genre. Certainly, as J.Z. Smith
observed ('Wisdom and Apocalyptic', in *Visionaries and their
Apocalypses*, ed. P.D. Hanson, London 1983, pp. 101-20),
apocalyptic/ism is a 'scribal phenomenon', essentially 'bookish'
in the methods of handling the message by writing it down
rather than communicating prophetically through the spoken
word. Of course such attitudes to texts as cryptic or revelatory
will outlast the period when the original literary genre
flourished.

The Literary Components of the Apocalypse of John

The exotic richness of Revelation lies in a diversity of literary
sub-forms that do not belong automatically to the genre of
apocalypse. These include:

> Autobiographical narratives of visions (from 1.9 onwards)
> Commissioning of a Prophet (1.17-19; 10.8–11.2)
> Prophetic oracles (1.7, 8; 13.9-10; 14.12-13; 16.15; 19.9-10;
> 21.5-8)
> Oaths (10.5-7)
> Plague sequences (chs. 6, 8 and 9, 16)
> Liturgical hymns (4.11; 5.9-14; 7.10-12, 15-17; 11.15-18;
> 12.10-12; 15.3-4; 16.5-7; 19.1-8) (There is also the
> possibility of longer liturgical structures underlying
> chs. 1, 4 and 5, 7 and 19)

Lamentations and dirges (18.2-24)
Woes (8.13)
Lists of virtues and vices (9.20-21; 14.4-5; 21.8, 27; 22.14-15) (Such lists, used for moral exhortation, technically known as catalogical paraenesis, are frequent in the Pauline letters—see 1 Thess. 4.1-12; Col. 3.5-17; Eph. 4.2-3, 17-24)
Letters (Cf. both the formal structures of the short letters in chs. 2 and 3 and the overall epistolary framework in chs. 1 and 22, with its opening and closing formulae [1.4-6; 22.21] and authority claims [1.1-3; 22.6-12, 16-20])

Lyle D. Vander Broek writes (in collaboration with James L. Bailey—*Literary Forms in the New Testament*, London 1992, p. 203),

> The exegete is called upon to recognise the uniqueness of these [literary sub-]forms in Revelation and to understand how they relate to the apocalyptic genre.

This unique relationship is easier to assert than to expound. To see the problem, one only has to consider the question, Which came first, the letter or the vision? The letter form provides the framework, but even the letters are given in a vision. But any commentator has a duty to hazard a guess as to why John employed this particular combination of literary materials.

The Integrity of the Work and its Structure

Among the older skills of literary criticism, the examination of sources and style in the Book of Revelation reached a peak with the two-volume commentary by R.H. Charles in the International Critical Commentary series (Edinburgh 1920). Twenty-five years of work produced a minute dissection of language and text, with the final chapters reordered and reconstructed, and many other passages assigned to an uncomprehending editor as later interpolations or meaningless survivals. In contrast, the second half of this century has seen a growing tendency to acknowledge the work's literary unity, while of course allowing for incongruities.

The modern reader notices a variety of structural devices which the author has employed to secure the literary unity of the work. The most important of these features are:

The sequences controlled by a significant number (such as seven or three). This principle of organization, repeated on three occasions in the sequences of plagues, allows for an element of recapitulation, while ensuring the progressive nature of the narrative. (Theories of total recapitulation overlook the distinctive character and purpose of each sequence, as well as the changing proportion of the world affected by the plagues.)

The deliberate interlocking of elements, with a sequence of three woes within the seven trumpets (chs. 8–11), or a bridging device (8.1-5) which relates seals and trumpets together.

The emphatic juxtapositions of triumph and tragedy, sequences of plagues and liturgical orders of praise (e.g. ch. 12). The deliberate contrast heightens the effect of both elements, while striving to preserve Christian hope in the darkest hour. From the perspectives of analytical psychology, this device may also relate to what Jung called 'coniunctio oppositorum', or the creation of a dialectical unity of opposites.

It is also important to investigate the possibilities of larger patterns of structural organization for the whole book. Perhaps one of the most useful and significant is a chiastic arrangement, such as is suggested by Elisabeth Schüssler Fiorenza (*The Book of Revelation: Justice and Judgment*, Philadelphia 1985, ch. 6):

A	1.1-8
B	1.9–3.22
C	4.1–9.21 + 11.15-19
D	10.1–11.14; 12.1–14.20 + 15.2-4
C'	15.1; 15.5–19.10
B'	19.11–22.9
A'	22.10-21

The positive effect of such a chiastic structure, where the sections with the same letters correspond to one another, is the focus given to the central section of the book (D) around which the rest is orientated. But for others the disadvantage inherent in this analysis is the obligation felt to chop up the text and reallocate sections, in order to make them fit the pattern. This can destroy some of the effective juxtapositions to which attention was drawn above.

But the real advantage rests in the principle underlying Elisabeth Schüssler Fiorenza's discussion of the literary structure.

> The early Christian apocalyptic tension between the now of the community and the eschatological future, between the 'already and not-yet' of the end-time, is expressed in the literary-structural tension between the forward-movement of the narrative, cyclic repetitions, and hymnic proclamations. The dramatic narrative of Revelation can best be envisioned as a conic spiral moving from the present to the eschatological future. It could also be likened to a dramatic motion-picture whose individual scenes portray the persons or actions every time from a different angle, while at the same time adding some new light or color to the whole (p. 7).

The principle involved is that a literary pattern can resemble a three-dimensional geometric figure, and this conveys a sense of the depth and of the perspectives within the book. In the same way a computer projection in the round would give a more adequate account than the flat contrasts of a semiotic square, or the simpler two-dimensional arrangement in patterns of sevens. In the end what is most important is that the reader should attempt to draw a route-map (with contour lines, to show height and depth!), and to offer a personal description of the journey through the book. The outline provided above at the beginning of Chapter 2 might serve as a starting point.

The Character of Revelation's Language

Everybody agrees that the Greek language in Revelation is peculiar. But there is widespread disagreement about the reasons for this. These are the main explanations:

1. It is essentially Greek, but barbaric, with deviations explained as a sloppiness or lack of competence, a deliberate flouting of the rules of syntax, or mistakes made because it is a second language. Parallels to these errors are claimed in the workaday vernacular language of the papyri found in Egypt.

2. The original apocalypse was written in Aramaic; the translation deliberately strives to reflect the original inspiration.

3. According to a nineteenth-century theory, this is a unique form of the language known only to the Holy Ghost ('Holy Ghost Greek').

4. According to a more critical perspective, it is 'biblical Greek', which betrays Hebrew influences as well as a continuity with the Septuagint (Greek translation of the Hebrew Bible). But why is Revelation more peculiar than other parts of the New Testament that are also in biblical Greek?

5. It is a first-century CE Jewish dialect of Greek, as used in Palestine ('distinguishable dialect of spoken and written Jewish Greek'—Nigel Turner; 'while he writes in Greek, he thinks in Hebrew'—R.H. Charles; 'Greek language...little more than a membrane, stretched tightly over a Semitic framework'—S. Thompson).

It may prove impossible to decide between these theories; but sharper definition and more precise analysis of the types of Greek found in the New Testament should be forthcoming from the more intensive computerized studies of the biblical language. The interpreter of Revelation, however, must also consider some of the implications of this use of the language. Was John his own secretary, since scribal resources might be limited in his Patmos prison? Was the choice of words his own, or was he influenced by apocalyptic conventions or a basic structure of formulaic composition? He could be writing the first large-scale Christian work of the apocalyptic genre, but would he have modelled himself deliberately on earlier Jewish traditions? Would this entail the use of archaic (and appropriately arcane) language? The fact that John does not follow

Daniel in adopting the convention of pseudonymity is not a decisive argument. The Christian revival of prophecy had transformed the situation in which the writer of Daniel had to use pseudonymity in order to key into the earlier Old Testament tradition of living prophecy. And John certainly does make use of Daniel for both his imagery and some of his literary sub-forms.

Author's Intention and Reader's Response

The modern emphasis is to examine a text from both perspectives, that is, to look not only at the way the author uses language, but also at the way that language would be understood. The need is to look for fruitful ways of describing the interaction between the author and the reader, and so to define the process of communication. We shall look at three possibilities that are not necessarily mutually exclusive.

1. *As an Interpretation of Tradition (Intertextuality)*
Austin Farrer (*Revelation*) emphasizes how important it is to understand John's book as a network of Old Testament exegesis:

> So far from reading like an attempt to communicate a previous visionary experience, the Revelation reads like a fresh and continuous scriptural meditation, conceived in the very words in which it is written down; as though, in fact, the author were thinking with his pen... He meditates into vision what he writes, and feels the presence of the mysteries he describes. But such vision can be achieved by a man working from words. The rabbis held that the most perilous technique of ecstasy was a meditation on the complicated text of Ezekiel's first chapter. St John takes the risk; in the fourth chapter of his Revelation he sees his way into heaven by the use of Ezekiel's and of several overlapping scriptural texts (pp. 24, 26).

Readers (both ancient and modern) need to be attuned to a select area of Old Testament texts as living traditions, which author and reader have in common, and from which creative interpretations can readily be made. Some may feel that a commentator like Austin Farrer strains credulity by the varied and intricate patterns of scriptural allusions proposed. But it is important not to neglect the possibility of any textual allusions or adopted symbols, so long as they are treated as options for exegesis rather than eisegetical controls. This can apply not only to the Old Testament but also to the use of themes from earlier Christian texts. The question of relative dating can be difficult here, but texts such as the Little Apocalypse (Mark 13 and parallels) could well be influential, even if its independent existence as a text of the apocalyptic genre is unproven.

A good model to consider for such Intertextuality is that cited above from J.-P. Ruiz (*Ezekiel in the Apocalypse*, Frankfurt 1989) in sequence D.6. in Chapter 2. He argues that John takes three motifs (prostitute, beast, city of Babylon) from his prophetic sources in Ezekiel, Daniel and Jeremiah. He blends them into a metaphoric unity in his vision, whereby this woman, animal and city must yield to another woman (the Church as the Bride of Christ) and another city (New Jerusalem), through the agency of another animal (the Lamb that was slaughtered).

As Gabriel Josipovici writes in *The Book of God* (New Haven 1988) p. 302:

> the biblical scribes worked within a living tradition, constantly transforming yet always remaining true to the spirit of the whole.

2. As Dramatic Performance (Orality and the Text)

This heading may be unexpected, given the emphasis of this chapter upon the literary character of the work. We can see how the act of writing is an important part of the book's authority. The command to 'write', for example, figures repeatedly in the literary sub-form of the prophetic oracle. And we have noted already that apocalyptic/ism is a 'scribal phenomenon', essentially 'bookish' in the methods of handling the message.

But with ancient texts we cannot exclude a spoken element on principle. Literature is linked to rhetoric by the fact that texts were often read aloud in the ancient world. With all the books in the New Testament it is likely that their written form is related to oral performance in public. This is not only to

echo the results of Form Criticism about the kerygmatic function of the units in the Synoptic Gospels; we must also think
of Paul's letters being read aloud to his churches, gathered for
worship. And David Aune has drawn attention to the unique
and innovative nature of Revelation (and the Shepherd of
Hermas) among apocalypses, because, he claims, they were
designed for dramatized performance:

> Orality played an explicit role in the composition of the
> Apocalypse of John, for the entire document was written
> expressly for public performance (Rev. 1.3; 22.18), and each of
> the seven proclamations of Rev. 2–3 are presented as dictated
> by the author, as are many other segments of the book (cf.
> Rev. 21.5). The fact that both the Apocalypse of John and the
> *Shepherd of Hermas* were intended for oral performance before
> Christian congregations *constitutes a unique feature of these two
> apocalypses* (*Semeia* 36, 1986, p. 78).

Certainly we can say that the literary genre of apocalypse is
modified significantly, even transformed, by the letter collection and the epistolary framework. The oral application of the
author's message may then be the explanation we sought
earlier for the unique combination of literary forms. This still
may seem to us like a nice irony. But it is important to recognize the continuing work of literary criticism in studying the
nature and the purpose of the interplay between oral and
written forms. It may have begun with studies in the Old
Testament prophets, or the early Christian prophetic revival,
but it does not end there. In Rev. 1.3 and 22.18 we have clear
evidence of essential parallelism between reading and hearing
in the use of a text. As some modern film-making has shown,
Revelation's symbols can be evoked with intense power in a
dramatic oral presentation. But perhaps we should think of an
ancient performance, with impersonal characteristics, like a
Greek tragedy using masks for the actors.

3. *As Symbol and Allegory*
Dionysius of Alexandria fiercely contested Revelation's place
in the New Testament canon. But he insisted that the book
had a non-literal meaning (although one beyond his compre-
hension!). He employed the techniques of literary criticism on

the seer's language to show that the Apocalypse was not written by John the Apostle, like the Gospel and the first Epistle of John. For this reason there was no question of preferring the symbolic meaning of Revelation, as a 'higher' meaning; indeed it should not be as highly regarded as the more literal, but apostolic, sense of the Gospel.

Nowadays, although there are still problems and prejudices about the place of the Apocalypse in the Canon, higher criticism has made us less positive about apostolic authorship and its implications. Writings in the tradition (school of thought) of Paul or John are not denied worth as Scripture for that reason. And we do not share unquestioningly the criteria, established by Origen in the patristic period, for an almost hierarchical scale of values: from literal up to symbolic/allegorical levels of moral and then spiritual meaning. A modern literary reading of the text may be attracted to the possibilities of allegory, but not because of any assumptions about the highest level of meaning.

But how is one to read apocalyptic images? Richard Bauckham ('The Figurae of John of Patmos', in *Prophecy and Millenarianism*, ed. A. Williams, Harlow 1980, p. 109) posed the question with this example:

> When we read in John's opening vision of the risen Christ that his head and his hair were white as white wool (Revelation 1.14) are we to visualize this feature as part of an attempt to share John's visual impression of the resplendent Son of Man? Or are we to treat it as a conventional item in literary descriptions of heavenly beings (cf. Apocalypse of Abraham II, of the archangel Jaoel)? Or are we to recall that in Daniel 7.9 this feature belongs not to the Son of Man but to the Ancient of Days, and so conclude that this reflects John's high Christology? Or should the white hair be allegorized as a symbol of Christ's eternal preexistence? Such questions cannot be finally answered without fuller studies than we have of the apocalyptists' use of imagery and John's specific relation to the apocalyptic tradition in this respect.

It should be obvious from a reading of Revelation that the author's imagery and symbolism are not all of a single kind. The differences are further indicated by the way John handles them. Some of the symbols are followed immediately by an interpretation which 'breaks the code' (see 1.20; 7.13-14; 12.9); but sometimes the solution may appear as cryptic as the problem (see 13.18; 17.9-18). Other symbols are more recognizable, traditional figures, perhaps even stereotypes (such as Babylon, Egypt, Jerusalem, Sodom); the reader brings prior familiarity with such echoes to assist in identification. Yet other symbols may capitalize on a certain familiarity in order to surprise and shock; they are used by the author, being deliberately stimulating and provocative, in a creative expansion of ideas (see the Lamb contrasted with the expected Lion in 5.5-6; and the relationship of parody between the riders of white horses at 6.2 and 19.11-16). Finally the author provides symbolic dream/visions of both heaven and the future, which may transcend all expectations (see chs. 4 and 21). And throughout the reader must remain open to the disconcerting possibilities that the same reality may be represented by more than one symbol, or that the same symbol may stand for more than a single reality.

It may be impossible to reach final conclusions on a particular symbol, as Richard Bauckham suggested above, through lack of data for comparison. But most commentators express personal preferences in their interpretations of the work as a whole. If there is a sliding scale—induced visionary experience; conventional but reworked allegorizing; traditional allegorical dream; remythologizing of imagery previously demythologized; symbolic vision—then most scholars would place John at the upper (and more creative) end of the scale. It is important not to underestimate the potency of symbolism. As Thomas Fawcett wrote in 1970 (before inclusive language was widely used):

> Man is confronted by a range of symbolic possibilities. The potential symbols in his experience determine the limits through which he can understand reality, and his receptiveness to these symbols determines his outlook. The history of man's use of symbols reflects his changing view of the universe and of his relationship to it. From this there emerges a most important characteristic of symbols, namely their power to direct our thinking and our orientation towards life (*The Symbolic Language of Religion*, London 1970, p. 32).

A striking visual image is a conceptual breakthrough. Skilled use of visual images is a means not only of expressing spiritual understanding but indeed of thinking theologically, by means of reflection upon the image and by further elaboration of its implications. To understand John's work fully, we need to be able to describe his process of seeing and writing. It may be that interpretations of Revelation also need to be visual.

4

FROM WHAT SETTING?
THE HISTORICAL AND SOCIAL
CONTEXT OF REVELATION'S COMMUNITY

FROM THE BEGINNINGS of modern biblical criticism until recently, historical investigations have occupied a dominant position. Open any academic commentary on a book of the New Testament and you are likely to find an early and substantial part of the introduction concerned with questions of date of writing, authorship and historical setting. The balance has shifted within the last decade; questions of literary structure, ways of reading, and methods of interpretation are asserting themselves and pushing the more historical questions into the background. So in the present work Chapter 3 precedes Chapter 4!

The real issue, however, is not the subject matter of the questions but their presuppositions. Are you (the readers) concerned solely with your action of reading—as if there were no yesterday and no tomorrow? Or are you reading to discover the intentions of the book in front of you—because these will resemble the intentions of the author, like a reflection in a mirror? Or are we together studying the text and using our basic training in biblical criticism to provide a window—so that we can look in at the original setting of the text in history, and the historical situation can signal its message to us indirectly, for us to apply its message analogously in our different/modern circumstances? The first two approaches use techniques of literary criticism, modern (post-modern!) and not-so-modern. The third is the approach of historical criticism, and this can apply to the criticism of source material as much as to the setting of the finished text.

Historical criticism may seem old-fashioned, but it is an essential method if we are to appreciate one important aspect of any primary apocalyptic text. There is an interrelationship between the text and the situation of crisis that produced it. The state of emergency affecting the community produces the text as a coded response, a theological evaluation of the real issues. But the text itself may well fuel the crisis, as it functions within the community setting as inflammatory propaganda. We are dealing with a literature of protest and revolt. It may counsel revolution, passive resistance or religious quietism. Clearly, then, we need to know as much as we can discover about the mutual relationship of the particular crisis and response.

Apocalypticism has proved a powerful catalyst for certain aspects of religious belief. To understand their importance what is needed is a description of the social world of a community in which an apocalyptic text is produced. It is then possible to apply sociological methods and comparative insights from anthropology to the texts and other historical evidence. What circumstances and what kind of communities are inclined to develop apocalyptic ideas? Perhaps an even more significant question is this: are there any precise analogies between the situations that nurtured Jewish and early Christian apocalyptic and the modern contexts (the nuclear threat, environmental concerns and feminism) in which apocalyptic language is ardently employed?

Questions of Dating

As I have observed elsewhere,

> a book whose business is 'revelation' has revealed little of the circumstances which produced it...*Revelation* comes from a situation of actual (or threatened) persecution of Christians by the local Roman imperial authorities in Asia Minor towards the end of the first century ('Revelation of John', *A Dictionary of Biblical Interpretation*, ed. R.J. Coggins and J.L. Houlden, London 1990, p. 593).

As to dating, there are some clues, both external and internal to the book, which we should notice, before considering how to reconstruct the social setting of John's communities.

Can we Trust the External Evidence?

The traditional date for the Apocalypse of John is in the reign of the emperor Domitian (81–96 CE). The basis for this is a remark of Irenaeus (*Adv. Haer.* 5.30.3):

> [the apocalyptic vision] was seen not such a long time ago, but almost in our generation, at the end of the reign of Domitian.

Other statements by Clement of Alexandria, Origen, Victorinus and Jerome are not necessarily independent of Irenaeus, and Eusebius quotes Irenaeus in his account of the Christian persecution under Domitian. Alternative datings, in the reigns of Trajan (98–117 CE), Nero (54–68 CE) or Claudius (41–54 CE), are late and may be based on misunderstandings.

> What Irenaeus says is straightforward, categorical, fairly precise and very credible. Domitian has always been remembered as a stereo-typically bad emperor; a persecutor who insisted on emperor-worship.

But Robert B. Moberly, from whom this last quotation comes, is not for that reason convinced. He doubts that we should place such reliance on Irenaeus' memory of what he had heard second-hand. It is not a standard date, fixed at the time in an established chronology, but a date constructed retrospectively (perhaps by totalling the reigns of emperors) where it is easy to stretch or foreshorten a span of time.

> Irenaeus was writing in Gaul, during the AD 180s or late AD 170s, about when an apocalyptic vision had been seen in Patmos...He thinks that John saw it 80–95 sketchily charted years earlier—in other words 35 sketchily charted years, or so, before he (Irenaeus) was born. We would not normally regard so distant, belated and second-hand an opinion as, by itself, evidence...Such opinions in Irenaeus are not, to my mind, necessarily false—or true. He presumably said what he had heard, at Smyrna in his boyhood, in (say) AD c. 140' (Moberly, 'When was Revelation Conceived?' *Biblica* 73/3, 1992, pp. 376, 381).

This means that the dating question cannot be settled by the external 'evidence'. At best we are offered clues to set alongside indications from the book itself. These may point collectively towards the traditional date under Domitian, or alternatively to a Trajanic date for the completion of a work begun under the Neronian persecution (as proposed by M. Hengel, *The Johannine Question*, London 1989, p. 81).

Internal Clues to the Dating

Revelation is preoccupied with the imminent collapse of the Roman Empire, the suffering and martyrdom of Christians as the result of persecution, and the problems of a blasphemous worship of the emperor. We cannot know whether any or all of these are present experiences or only realistic expectations at the time of writing. There are limited periods in the first century of the Church's life in which these were realities, but not necessarily all at the same time. Otherwise we may be dealing with vivid, and credible, imaginings. What has already been said about the literary unity of the work, might cause hesitation before we argue for an apocalypse composed in stages. Only if literary and historical arguments combine is this more than a solution of last resort, or a sign of well-edited source materials. Here is a summary of the positive aspects in favour of four times (in reverse chronological order) when Christians experienced or feared persecution from Rome.

1.*The Reign of Trajan*
Only at this time is there clear evidence for the persecution of Christians in Asia Minor, documented in the exchange of letters between the younger Pliny and the emperor Trajan c. 112 CE (Pliny *Ep*. X. 96-97). Pliny seems the complete caricature of a civil servant needing to consult the emperor on every decision; but we should be grateful because of the information he gives us about the issues involved.

> [Those who denied they were Christians] recited a prayer to the
> gods at my dictation, made supplication with incense and wine
> to your statue, which I had ordered to be brought into court for

the purpose together with the images of the gods, and moreover cursed Christ—things which (so it is said) those who are really Christians cannot be made to do.

[Those who ceased to be Christians] maintained, however, that the amount of their fault or error had been this, that it was their habit on a fixed day [cf. Rev. 1.10] to assemble before daylight and recite by turns a form of words to Christ as a god; and that they bound themselves with an oath [*sacramentum*]... After this was done, their custom was to depart, and to meet again to take food, but ordinary and harmless food.

Christianity has evidently spread rapidly in this part of Asia, so as to be a problem. There are anxieties about the effect on pagan cults, as well as emperor worship; the situation resembles that of Ephesus in Acts 19. All kinds of popular accusations against the Christians were current (such as arson, incest, ritual cannibalism). Counter-evidence is taken from two women deacons under torture (as happened with slaves' evidence under Roman law). The Christians held two meetings on a Sunday: the first an early service probably for the sacrament (Pliny misunderstands the term as taking an oath); the second is an 'Agape' or fellowship meal. The crucial test in these trials is the refusal of Christians to venerate pagan images, or even to demonstrate their loyalty by paying divine honours to the emperor. In reply Trajan cites no precedent to guide Pliny in knowing how far to pursue the Christians. Christianity is not yet an explicit offence on the statute book, but rather a matter for summary police action if a situation becomes dangerous. Tertullian later complained that Trajan's ruling was inconsistent: 'He says they must not be ferreted out, as though they were innocent; he orders them to be punished, as though they were guilty!'

The Apocalypse was completed or reworked early in the reign of Trajan, according to Martin Hengel in his discussion of *The Johannine Question*:

The Apocalypse could be an earlier work, the nucleus of which was written in the time after the shock of the Neronian persecution, the beginning of the Judaean war, the murder of Nero and the civil war; possibly it was reworked later, early in the reign of Trajan, by a pupil who depicted the elder as a recipient of apocalyptic revelation and a prophet (p. 81).

John the Elder was 'a real historical personality, a teacher and charismatic authority who worked in the Flavian period and early in the reign of Trajan in Ephesus and founded a school there'. Although the basis of the book was his experience in exile on Patmos, the final form of the work reflects later and different perspectives. The arguments for the later date have more to do with the total span of Hengel's theory than with any specific internal evidence. Time is needed for improvement in the Greek and change to a more conservative outlook (there are similarities between the seven letters and 1 John). Is it a pupil's viewpoint to depict John in Revelation as a Christian prophet, outside the group of twelve apostolic authorities of the past (see Rev. 21.14)? But the principal evidence for the time of Trajan is a working back through the Johannine tradition in Asia Minor, from Polycrates of Ephesus and Irenaeus, via Polycarp of Smyrna to Papias of Hierapolis, writing about a generation after John the Elder himself.

2. *The Reign of Domitian*

There is very little firm evidence for the persecution of Christians under Domitian, despite his notorious reputation. Dio Cassius and Suetonius both record the death of Flavius Clemens, among others in 96 CE. Dio says that Clemens and his wife Domitilla were accused of 'atheism' and 'Jewish customs'—which could mean Christianity, but is hardly conclusive. Clemens is not to be identified with Clement, bishop of Rome and author of *1 Clement* (often dated to Domitian's reign), which speaks of 'sudden and repeated misfortunes and calamities' and 'unexpected and repeated troubles' (1.1). Brian W. Jones (*The Emperor Domitian*, London 1992, pp. 114-15) writes,

> Just possibly, the phrases in question might refer to prominent Christian sympathizers denounced by informers late in the 90s: three or four executed or banished could well have represented a calamity to a comparatively small group.

It is all a question of scale and significance; but the fact remains that

No pagan writer accused Domitian of persecuting Christians,
though Nero's activities in this regard were recorded as was
Domitian's determination to tax the Jews.

Christian tradition of Domitian as a persecutor grew quite
rapidly. Eusebius quotes both Melito of Sardis (c. 170 CE) as
saying that evil advisers persuaded Nero and Domitian to
slander Christian teaching, and Tertullian as claiming a little
later that Domitian 'almost equalled Nero in cruelty, but,
because he had some commonsense, he soon stopped what he
had begun and recalled those he had exiled' (*Hist. Eccl.* 3.20;
4.26). It is Eusebius who includes Domitian's banishment of
John to Patmos in his *Chronicorum Canonum*. Domitilla is
reckoned as a Christian, but instead of being the wife of
Flavius Clemens and mother of his seven children, she has
become his virgin niece; the second-century Christian catacomb
in Rome named after Domitilla may reflect the growing tradition or merely the original ownership of the land.

Domitian's bad reputation certainly results from his enthu-
siasm for making the cult of the emperor compulsory, even in
Rome and the west as well as in the east (cf. Rev. 13.11-17;
20.4). He revelled in his relationship to the newly deified
emperors Vespasian and Titus. A temple to Domitian and his
deified relatives was dedicated at Ephesus in the year 89/90
CE, and S.R.F. Price (*Rituals and Power*, Cambridge 1984,
pp. 197-98) believes this was the occasion that prompted John
to write. Suetonius also tells the story of Domitian's dictating a
circular letter to be used by the procurators beginning 'Our
Lord and God commands this to be done' (*Dominus ac deus
noster...*—cf. Jn 20.28). But in the end Domitian was assas-
sinated and not deified.

3. *The Reign of Titus*
Although Suetonius called Titus 'the delight and darling of
the human race' and recorded the spontaneous mourning and
affection that greeted his early death in 81 CE, yet his
accession in 79 CE on the death of his father, Vespasian, had
been dreaded because of earlier glimpses he had given of his
real character. His concessions to the Senate, and a policy of
mild tolerance, failed to stop the spread of discontent, especi-

ally in the East. The Jews were ready to ascribe an agonizing end to the actual person who had destroyed the temple in Jerusalem (cf. Rev. 11.2). According to Sulpicius Severus, Titus had reflected that to destroy the Temple

> would be an invaluable way of doing away with both the Christian and the Jewish religions, for, although mutually inimical, these two faiths had sprung from the same root... and, once the root was dug up, the stem would soon perish.
>
> (*Chronicle* 2.30.6)

Dio Cassius records that a false Nero appeared in the reign of Titus; there may have been more than one of these impostors appearing at this time in Asia Minor, giving fresh impetus to the legend that Nero must return (*Redivivus*—after his suicide in 68 CE) at the head of a Parthian army to regain his throne (see Rev. 13.3; 17.8, 11). 'Nero Redivivus' rapidly becomes a symbol of renewed civil war for Rome and an eschatological omen. If Nero is appropriately the first of the sequence of seven heads (17.9), then the sixth who is now reigning (17.10) is Titus. Current expectations and fears centre upon Titus' brother Domitian who has been designated as the next emperor. Domitian must not reign long, if the Church and Rome are to survive. For into the reign of the seventh emperor the diabolical eighth ('Nero Redivivus') will irrupt as a ghastly and catastrophic climax. If the riddle of the beast is correctly solved in this way, an amazingly precise date (within three years) has been achieved for this central focus of the Apocalypse, and therefore possibly for the whole book.

4. *The Year of the Four Emperors*
Robert B. Moberly (*Biblica* 73/3, 1992, pp. 376-93) is the most recent writer to make a case for Revelation (or its main vision) as a response to one particular year of crisis for the Roman empire. 69 CE was the year, following Nero's suicide, in which Galba, Otho and Vitellius struggled in turn to hold power, and from which Vespasian emerged victorious. Rome, personified as the goddess Roma and satirized as Babylon, is on the point of collapse from civil warfare. This does justice to the sense, throughout Rev. 16.17–19.2, of an imminent fall.

Although Rome was in control of much of the world, this year was, in Tacitus' words, 'nearly the final year of the state'. With the fall of Otho, the number of Caesars who had died violently and bloodily (at their own or another's hand) could be calculated at five: Julius Caesar, Gaius (Caligula), Nero, Galba and Otho. The intervals between their deaths have become dramatically shorter. Vitellius is now the 'sixth' (see Rev. 17.10) reigning as emperor with help from the legions of Gaul, Upper and Lower Germany and Britain—four out of the (approximately) 'ten' armies of Rome (see 17.12). The other six acclaimed Vespasian in July 69, so that a final confrontation between Vitellius and Vespasian appeared imminent. It might be that Nero Redivivus would return from Parthia to play a part in Rome's downfall.

The recollection of the historical Nero is still vivid. The recent fact of Christian martyrdoms, in the ghastly public spectacle orchestrated by Nero (Tacitus *Annals* 15.44—see sequence B.6 in Chapter 2 above), would help to explain Revelation's preoccupation with justice and vengeance (see 6.9-10). Depending on the date of the Neronian persecution (64, 65, or 66 CE), the interval between the first martyrdoms and the Year of the Four Emperors could be three and a half years (see 11.2; 12.6, 14; 13.5). If so, then the symbolic time has a very precise and literal reference. Also these were years in which (Moberly thinks) Jews and Christians shared a common grievance against Rome, and so interreligious animosity is not reflected in the main part of the Apocalypse. Certainly this dating comes between the Jewish revolt in 66 CE and the fall of Jerusalem in 70 CE; so the temple is still standing and can be measured (see 11.1).

A case is therefore argued for an apocalyptic work conceived in rapid response to oral reports of the events in this year, as the garbled set of impressions reached Patmos before winter made travel impossible. It must be debated whether information of sufficient accuracy for the scenario in Revelation would have reached an isolated exile this quickly, and whether the author had the practical resources on the island to produce even a first draft of his work.

Are any of These Internal Indications Conclusive?

The evidence for any one of these four datings is cumulative but still not overwhelming. It may amount to no more than circumstantial evidence! It is an irony, frequently observed, that John's clues to the time of writing can afford to be so enigmatic, because his first recipients knew as well as he the situation for which he wrote. Only the first and last solutions offer firm evidence of persecution of Christians, because of the doubt about Domitian. The second has the benefit of external support from Irenaeus, if this can be trusted. The third, with its memories and fears about Titus, still makes good sense in a 'Jewish' apocalyptic milieu. But the earlier the date is set, the harder it is to allow for the highly developed use of traditional motifs in the book. In the late sixties or early seventies CE, it is more likely that Babylon stands for Jerusalem rather than Rome. But most commentators have difficulty with a proposal such as that of J.M. Ford (*Revelation*, Anchor Bible, New York 1975)—a Jerusalem-orientated revelation to John the Baptist. The majority are convinced that Babylon is Rome or Roma.

If an early date still appeals, it would be better to consider the possibility of source materials and traditions, formulated in response to events, just as the material of Mark 13 may have been produced in Caligula's day, but then assimilated fairly thoroughly into a later work. So Christian thinking about the Roman empire in, say, the last decade of the first century would be highly coloured by the experiences and attitudes of an earlier generation of Christians. Students of apocalyptic are very aware of how much material is recycled (perhaps repeatedly) from earlier contexts. One therefore looks at the material on two levels: (1) the traces of origins reflected in pieces of the text; and (2) the overall perspectives of the final version. This final version may have a literary (and dramatic) integrity, while indicating that some ingredients (e.g. chs. 11 and 12) belong to an earlier generation and have therefore now been given a retrospective character, presented as a 'flashback'.

Reconstructing the Social Setting of John's Community

There are two methods of approach to this task: to move from theory to practice, or vice versa. Most attempts have started from a social theory and sought to match the data of the Apocalypse to the theory. The danger is that a preferred model will simply be imposed. Alternatively to start from specific indications in Revelation runs the risk that evidence will point in several directions (as with the question of dating) and no single theory will result.

Engels, writing about 'Revelation' in 1883 within the Marx–Engels collaboration *On Religion*, popularized the work of German Protestant biblical scholars and argued that Revelation was the earliest extant text of Christianity. The Apocalypse gave an authentic picture of the primitive Christian community as a more or less revolutionary group (part of the revolution of the masses). The evidence was that John showed clear signs of class hatred, a vengeful attitude against Rome and against the ideology of the oppressive class. Clearly such an interpretation is indebted to the model of socialist movements, as much as to the biblical evidence.

More recent sociological theory frequently applies the model of the sect to apocalyptic writing in general. Revelation corresponds closely to the pattern of a Jewish and Christian literary genre and therefore should show a sectarian group, marginalized by the attitudes of mainstream society. To some extent this model is also a reading back from the experience of much more recent groups who have used Revelation, from the Puritans of New England, and Edward Irving, the hell-fire preacher and founder of the Catholic Apostolic Church, to the millenarian sects studied by contemporary anthropologists; because of this the results must be treated with caution. The theory of cognitive dissonance (beautifully illustrated in the novel by Alison Lurie, *Imaginary Friends*, London 1967/1987) is often applied to such groups, to explain why they survive long after their original prophecies of the end have failed. Such disappointment, which might be expected to lead to the group's disintegration, is apparently overcome by a revised message, antinomianism, and increased missionary activity in compensation.

The dilemma of the social scientist, particularly with regard to religious movements in modern society, but also with their ancient parallels, is to know if the proliferation of sectarian movements indicates a revival of the religious spirit or a deterioration in the face of social pressures. Social scientists are primarily concerned with any religion's outward forms and structures; their criteria are quantitative rather than qualitative. And so their theoretical interpretations are unavoidably limited. If a dialogue between theological and sociological interpretation is possible, it is much more likely to produce comprehensive results.

Evidence from the Text of Revelation

John's community is clearly under severe stress, although not necessarily official persecution by the Roman authorities. Persecution in the first century, as we have seen, was localized and spasmodic, at the provocation of informers, rather than a regular process with an established legal base. But certainly the community faced ostracism and social contempt. They feel threatened and insecure, and must contend with religious as well as social stress. This stress is produced in the first place by the externally enforced worship of the Roman Emperor, with social and economic sanctions applied against non-conformists. Ruler cults were a long-established and politically valuable principle in Asia Minor. In the Roman Empire, the east urged the familiar idea out of tribute and loyalty; the west reluctantly conformed when coerced by an enthusiastic emperor. But there is also some evidence in Revelation for another kind of religious stress which arises from internal religious conflicts. These are represented symbolically in the text by cryptic references to opponents of the churches, called the Nicolaitans (2.6, 15) and the synagogue of Satan (2.9)—possibly also by Balaam (2.14) and Jezebel (2.20) as alternative prophetic voices to the Seer's.

A comparison between the Gospel of John and the Apocalypse reveals a surprising difference in the nature of

their religious communities. In the gospel the group appears
to be enclosed and inward-looking, a community of believers
ultimately liberated from this world and its constraints (see
Jn 17). But in Revelation the community is not closed like the
stereotype of the apocalyptic sect. Instead it is a group with a
very positive sense of mission to the world. It is possible to see
this as one of the results of the process of Cognitive
Dissonance (see above), on the assumption that the gospel
pre-dates Revelation in the same community. But a contrasting interpretation is more likely, given the depth of the
positive attitude to mission throughout the traditions of
Revelation. Rev. 7.2-4 does speak of 144,000 who are 'sealed'
and protected like an elect; but it should be read as a symbolic
number, modelled on Israel in the Old Testament, whose task
it is to inspire and lead to salvation an infinitely larger
number of people from the whole world (see 7.9-14; 5.9-10;
14.6). In ch. 15 the symbolic transition is at its most effective:
the song of Moses (Old Testament) becomes the song of the
Lamb (New Testament); and the 144,000 (15.2 = 14.1-2)
become an infinite number with participation now open to the
world (15.4).

A key idea for mission in Revelation is 'witness' (which is
the same Greek word as 'martyrdom'). The visions of ch. 11,
describing the fate of 'my two witnesses', indicate how this act
of Christian 'witnessing' and mission is ultimately effective.
'Witness' is therefore defined as communicating the gospel
message in the context of a fundamentally prophetic
community. Witness is an activity undertaken in the closest
relationship to Christ, on the path from suffering to glory (1.5;
11.8). God's reign is seen as being universal in scope, but
working towards its fullest realization through human agencies and representative individuals. The prevailing situation
in the world is such that acts of witness often entail the completion of Christian testimony by martyrdom.

The situation as depicted is that of cosmic confrontation; the
powers of evil ranged against God's purposes for the world are
no mere phantoms. The task of Christian prophecy, which in
part inherits the mantle of the Old Testament prophets and
the negative response they came to expect, is to present the

gospel to the world and offer the occasion for repentance and change of heart. The prophetic figure and his or her community may feel isolated and vulnerable, but the witness can be confident of speaking with God-given authority. The way the group conducts itself is a powerful symbol and a testimony to the world.

'The Book of Revelation struggles to speak for the whole world; yet if it lost its minority status, it would lose its raison d'etre.' Leonard L. Thompson seeks in this way a broader social base for the book at the end of his 'dramatic' presentation (*The Book of Revelation—Apocalypse and Empire*, New York 1990). He rightly resists the ideological tendency to find for Revelation a narrowly defined social location, determined solely by political or economic factors affecting a marginalized sect; this is to ignore the wider appeal of Revelation's language in ancient as in modern times. But it cannot speak for the public order of the status quo without ceasing to be an apocalypse. There is an 'ambivalent relationship with the larger order' so that the book can be accepted 'without relocating into a sect-type social base'. All that is required is for the larger order of society to be 'engaged as the enemy from a particular Christian perspective'.

> John and his audience can, however, be located in Roman society as a group of people who understand themselves as a minority that continuously encounters and attacks the larger Christian community and the even larger Roman social order. That communal self-understanding leads us back to the paradox of a 'cosmopolitan sectarianism'. The universal, cosmic vision of the Book of Revelation is grounded in first-century Asian life and necessarily entangles itself in all power structures in all dimensions of human society. But it entangles itself as opposition. It opposes the public order and enters the fray as other 'deviant' groups in the empire, not by joining rioters in the streets but by a literary vehicle, a written genre—in John's case, a genre offering revealed knowledge as an alternative to the knowledge derived from the public order (pp. 195-96).

Thompson emphasizes the importance of the communication of revealed knowledge as a basic clue to the book's social setting. But his broader approach must not be seen as emptying the Apocalypse of specific reference and allowing it to be 'all things to all people'. The epistolary framework of the book and, even more, the seven letters it contains are essential to the aim of 'direct communication'. Detailed symbolism in the letters links back to the vision of Christ who is the author of the communication, and forward to the vision of hope in the New Jerusalem. And these letters tell us specific facts about the local communities and what may be 'house churches' set up by John in these cities. The religious tensions with the Seer's opponents within the Christian churches are an important aspect of the social situation. As Martin Hengel suggests (see above), the issues and rivalries may be comparable with those reflected in the canonical letters—1–3 John. But the range of other social details needs to be studied, with Colin J. Hemer's *The Letters to the Seven Churches* as an informative guide. These seven letters afford valued glimpses of John's communities and show how the message of the Apocalypse is grounded in the historical realities of the churches.

THE ABIDING THEOLOGICAL VALUES AND DOCTRINES OF REVELATION

How Jewish is the Theology of Revelation?

HOW THE RELATIONSHIP between Christianity and Judaism is reflected in the Apocalypse remains one of the most tantalizing of historical problems, while it is of the greatest theological significance. Most scholars are now much less confident about dating the so-called 'Parting of the Ways' to the last decades of the first century. It used to be thought that the additional formulation in the Eighteen Benedictions of Judaism—a curse upon the Minim, or heretics—applied solely to the Christians and showed how wide the gap had become. Even if this were so, it is not necessarily reflected in John's Gospel with its reference to excommunication from the synagogue at 9.22 and 12.42. The Apocalypse is related to the Gospel in a number of respects, some problematic, but its own relationship to Judaism shows little sign of the open confrontation found in the Gospel (e.g. Jn 8). It is not just that Revelation makes use of an originally Jewish literary genre (apocalypse). There also seems to be a positive role ascribed to Israel as the mother of the Messiah in Revelation 12—at least as positive as Paul's hopes for Israel in Romans 9–11. And there is no reason to suppose that remarks about 'a synagogue of Satan' (2.9; 3.9) are less symbolic, and therefore more anti-Semitic, than the denunciation of Jezebel the prophetess. Indeed, so Jewish has the Apocalypse appeared to be that Rudolf Bultmann, for example, could claim that the faith of Revelation was a Judaism which had only been slightly

Christianized (*Theology of the New Testament*, London 1975, II, p. 175).

Nevertheless the flight of the Jewish Christians to Pella, in the course of the Jewish War (which could be represented symbolically in Revelation 12.14-16), might well have been regarded by the Jews as an act of treachery, deserting their Jewish compatriots in the hour when solidarity was needed. This could have provoked the Jewish synagogue reaction after the War, culminating in the expulsion associated with the Birkat ha-Minim. But if earlier 'persecution' of Jewish Christians by Jews had been more intense (as may be reflected in 1 Thess. 2.14), then the practical boundaries had been drawn already, and the Christian withdrawal from Jerusalem was scarcely surprising.

Alan F. Segal in his comparison of Judaism and Christianity in the Roman world *Rebecca's Children* (Harvard 1986, pp. 130-31) writes of the variety of responses among both Jewish and Christian groups to the historical fact of the fall of the Jerusalem temple in 70 CE:

> Each different Christian community designed a response to the destruction of the Temple to fit its own interpretation of history. Within Christianity the Temple characteristically became either the body of Christ, the church, or the Christian community itself. Later Christianity used the passion of Jesus as justification for an end to the entire sacrificial cult. Jesus' sacrifice on the cross became the perfect sacrifice of the perfect priest on the perfect altar...[the Letter to the Hebrews]. In the Revelation of John...the new world envisioned at the end of time becomes a new Jerusalem but not a new Temple.

The key questions to ask, in response to Segal, are whether Revelation sees Christ's death fully in terms of the Jewish sacrificial system; and is the Temple missing from the New Jerusalem because it is superseded, or because its theological importance is realized in more spiritual terms (21.22), as was the case with the Pharisaic realization of Rabbinic Judaism after 70 CE?

Once again we are being offered not only such polarized alternatives in the interpretation of Revelation (independent-minded Christianity or a Jewish-Christian tradition) but also the possibility of a range of intermediate points on a sliding scale. We cannot resolve such matters in isolation, but we need to compare a whole range of theological issues. Not only are these important in determining the preponderance of theological concerns in Revelation, but they will also help us to establish how revolutionary the Apocalypse is in theological matters and therefore how provocative this book can be for future generations of readers, including ourselves. The topics we shall examine are these:

> The person of Christ
> The work of Christ
> The doctrine of God
> The work of the Holy Spirit

1. *The Person of Christ*

Margaret Barker's perspectives on Old Testament and Inter-testamental theology are original, speculative and much debated by scholars. But her discussion of evidence from Revelation for the picture of Christ as 'the Great Angel' help-fully focuses our attention on the key issues:

> The first Christians identified Jesus with the Great Angel not only in their reading of the Old Testament but also in their new writings... The prologue to Revelation is the earliest detailed recognition of Jesus as the Great Angel. Both the description and the setting are unmistakable. The Angel was a human figure with flaming eyes and feet like burnished bronze, appearing in the temple. He was in the midst of the seven lampstands, meaning, surely, not that he stood among seven separate lamps but that he was the central stem of the sevenfold lamp, as Philo's Logos had been [*Rev. Div. Her.* 215]. He introduced himself as Yahweh: 'I am the first and the last and the living one' (Rev. 1.17), with which we should compare [Isa. 44.6; 48.12-13]... The Angel of John's vision was the one whom Isaiah had called Yahweh, the Redeemer of Israel (*The Great Angel* London 1992, pp. 200-201).

The figure is clearly Jesus, by virtue of the Resurrection (2.8). Yet, like Yahweh of the Old Testament, he permits people to eat from the tree of life (2.7), and he has the sword of judgment (2.12). The title 'Amen' in 3.14 might be a corruption of 'Amon' the heavenly master workman (= Wisdom in Prov. 8.30). The Lamb in 5.6 has seven eyes, as the eyes of Yahweh

in Zech. 4.10. The Christ figure rides from heaven as the
warrior judge (19.11-14—see Deut. 32.43). He treads the
winepress of wrath (19.15—see Isa. 63.3-6). Jerusalem was the
bride of Yahweh (Isa. 54) and so is the bride of Christ (Rev.
21). For these and other reasons (especially the use of the
temple motifs as a setting) Margaret Barker concludes:

> *There can be no doubt that for John the heavenly Christ was the
> ancient Yahweh* [emphasis hers]. Revelation had a temple set-
> ting for the son of man/lamb/angel figure; the great judgement
> was a heavenly liturgy spilling over onto the earth (p. 203).

On this evidence the angel language of Revelation is either
very sophisticated, with its resonances creating an advanced
or 'exalted' Christology (on the way to Chalcedon), or it is a
quite undeveloped and 'low' Christology, with Christ seen as
an angel (a heavenly being functioning as a messenger or
intermediary for God). Just possibly it is a mixture of both, as
one particular tradition of Christianity searches for ways to
express its faith. We must not conclude that the theology is
undeveloped because the mode of expression is alien and
sounds unsophisticated to us. To speak of Christ as an angel
may not seem to be saying much about his relation to God.
But this angelic figure at least controls and sends other angels
(1.1; 22.16). Yet the Christology of the Letter to the Hebrews,
with its apparently strong Jewish colouring, asserts the
superiority of Christ to any angel in the first chapter. Would
the writer of Revelation have agreed?

The parallelism between the visions in Revelation 4 and 5
gives us the impression that the worship of heaven is jointly of
God (as the one seated on the throne) and of the Lamb. This
impression is maintained later in the book (e.g. 21.22; 22.1):
the joint presence of God and the Lamb functions as the
equivalent of the temple (the symbol of God's presence) for the
New Jerusalem. The Lamb is worshipped because of what he
has done (victory achieved in some way by his death—see
below on the work of Christ). He has already fulfilled the
divine plan for salvation; the acclamation and ascription of
divine honours to him now match the hymn to God himself
(5.9; see 4.11). He now has the status deserving of worship; it
is not said whether he had it before his victory. He is uniquely

worthy to take the scroll from the right hand of God and reveal the future.

The Lamb first appears (at 5.6) 'between the throne and the four living creatures and among the elders'. If the four living creatures (in the tradition of Ezek. 1.5-14) are four fiery aspects of the glory of God, then the Lamb is included within the aura of the Godhead. But the Lamb is also 'among the elders' who are usually taken to be the patriarchal and apostolic representatives of the Old and New Testaments. If there is any precision in the choreography of this heavenly vision, then the Lamb's relationship to the elders could represent his function through the whole history of salvation, as God's link with humanity, rather than classifying the nature of the Lamb as human, not divine. To take the option of a more exalted Christology makes an attractive link with the later arguments of Irenaeus. He interpreted the four living creatures as 'images of the dispensation of the Son of God'. So God is revealed to the four corners of the world by means of the four canonical gospels. And so from this point it was appropriate to identify the four creatures as symbols of the four evangelists.

It is possible to defend a similar or stronger continuity within the writings of the Johannine circle from which both Revelation and the Gospel of John are claimed to originate. W. Grundmann (*Der Zeuge der Wahrheit*, Berlin 1985, pp. 59, 70) argued that two out of the four main features of the Fourth Gospel's view of Christ have their roots in Revelation. The structured sequence of seven 'I am' sayings has its starting point in Revelation 1.8, 17-18: 'I am the Alpha and the Omega...I am the first and the last, and the living one. I was dead, and see, I am alive forever and ever.' The 'I am' formula of Johannine theological statement begins as an oracular form of self-disclosure in the Apocalypse, where it functions 'to legitimate the revealer and the revelations which follow' (D. Aune, *Semeia* 36, 1986, p. 84). In the same way the theme of Christ as 'witness of Truth' originates with the testimony of 'Christ the faithful witness' (1.2, 5). (For more on this theme see below, under Holy Spirit).

2. *The Work of Christ*

Great care is needed, not only to describe the work of Christ in terms which Revelation uses, but also to allow for the thought-world where the imagery is used. Geza Vermes has observed recently:

> As anyone familiar with late Second Temple Jewish literature knows, warlike imagery is part of the apocalyptic style, but it does not necessarily entail violent political action, any more than the bloody metaphors in the description of the rider on the white horse (Rev. 19) would suggest that the early Church conceived of the returning Messiah as a cruel war-lord (*TLS* 4.12.1992).

In the Apocalypse Christ performs (in past, present and future) a wide range of tasks, from communicating prophetic revelation (1.1-2, 5, 19) to riding on a white horse so as to judge and make war (19.11-13). But, in systematic theology, discussions of the work of Christ tend to focus on the purpose and results of the death of Christ. There are certainly a large number of references in the book to Christ, the Lamb's, act of dying. But we must be careful not to jump to conclusions about what they mean, like some commentators who fill up what is lacking in Revelation by echoes of Paul's language in Romans or elsewhere! This extract from Graeme Goldsworthy *The Gospel in Revelation* (pp. 30, 47), commenting on 1.5-6; 5.5-6; 7.13-14, illustrates the danger:

> The Lion is the image of the glorified and reigning Christ. He alone can unlock the kingdom of God to us and make its reality known. But, like John, we can see the Lion only as he has come to us in the form of the slain Lamb. John points to the gospel-event; the living, dying and rising of Jesus Christ, as the key to the revelation of the kingdom. It is thus also the key to the Book of Revelation... When we speak of justification we are using a formal or technical way of referring to the gospel and its meaning. Through the life and death of Jesus the believer is accounted by God as free from the guilt of sin, and is thus accepted by God as his child. It is this message that permeates all that John is saying to us in Revelation. We note that it was the preaching of this gospel which led to the occasion for the writing of Revelation [Rev. 1.9].

Kenneth Grayston (*Dying We Live*, London 1990) certainly avoids this pitfall. He has no wish to assimilate John's thought to the authentic views of Paul, his preferred interpreter of the death of Christ. He argues that the emphasis on the Lamb's dying is in Revelation for quite a different purpose, essentially as a call for vengeance and the means of achieving it:

> The author of Revelation is not embarrassed by the death of Christ and has no intention of excusing it, defending it, or explaining it away. Instead he uses it to attack the social and political structures of his day. The slain Lamb stands before the divine court and relentlessly accuses Roman society for its ill treatment of God's people and its radical disturbance of mankind and the world. The author of Revelation, in fact, adopts and revises an old perception of Christ's death, namely, as a protective device that turns away evil. The powers of evil cannot easily be restrained, and the saints must suffer as Christ had suffered; but they are not abandoned, they will not go unavenged, and their time of dominance will come. Shed blood calls for vengeance, and vengeance will soon fall upon those who are not written in the Lamb's book of life. In the great conflict between the creative powers of the heavenly world and the destructive powers of the abyss everything turns on the martyrdom of Christ—even when the author allows his imagination to run wild with bitter images of catastrophe and chaos. In the end, shed blood makes no further demands. The theme is life. There is new heaven and a new earth. The marriage of the Lamb to his bride is foreseen, and trees are planted for feeding and healing the nations (p. 358).

The message of Revelation about the death of Christ probably lies between these two extremes of interpretation. Even the language of 1.5-6 is not exactly what Paul would have said; it lacks the historical particularity of one sacrifice completely effected as a demonstration of God's love. On the other hand Kenneth Grayston's conclusion (summarized by one reviewer as 'the Apocalypse, despite the central image of the slaughtered Lamb, lapses into unselfcritical vindictiveness'!—John Muddiman in *Church Times* 8.3.1991) scarcely does justice to the sympathetic appraisal of Revelation in his exegesis. The theme of the Passover lamb may be present in ch. 5, and we have no reason for devaluing the sacrificial language by

describing it as merely traditional. The Lamb—'standing as if
it had been slaughtered'—is 'intelligible if understood as indicating an unblemished male, wholly devoted in sacrifice to God
(following the standard rules for choosing and offering the
whole burnt offering)'. The 'sacrificial blood was an apotropaic
rite [protective device] against the destructive forces unleashed
by God' (p. 328). Even more significantly, 'John is asserting
that the death of Christ is...a constitutive act for the created
order and human history' (p. 332). It seems to me that it is the
creative attempt to translate the death of Christ into a sacrifice
of cosmic significance, supremely relevant to world problems
as we know them, that is the distinctive contribution made by
Revelation to understanding the work of Christ.

3. *The Doctrine of God*
The basis of Revelation's thought about God is given expression in the traditional language of the Old Testament
prophets. So God is the holy and righteous judge whom the
whole world should hold in awe. God's word can be heard, but
God himself cannot be seen. As in Isaiah 6 what is seen, even
in the holiest of this world's perspectives, the liturgical experience in the Temple, is only 'the hem of his robe', the point at
which this world is touched by God's glorious otherness. It is
therefore appropriate that the seer often echoes the mystical
language of Ezekiel, especially the esoteric symbolism of
Ezekiel 1–3.

It is equally in the tradition of Daniel and other apocalyptic
texts that Revelation has a dynamic concept of God as one
who intervenes ultimately and decisively for both salvation
and judgment. These apocalypses share with Old Testament
prophecy a belief in the directness of divine intervention in
human affairs; where they differ is in the sense of the scale
required. For the apocalyptist, the world is in such desperate
straits that only a cosmic intervention will save anyone.
Although it is not referred to specifically in the text, the appropriate model would be the Great Flood of Genesis 6–9. The
prime purpose is judgment, for the 'wickedness of humankind
was great in the earth' (Gen. 6.5). But Noah and his family are
rescued and blessed. In this saving act God establishes his

'covenant...that never again shall there be a flood to destroy the earth' (9.11). In the same way Revelation uses the Exodus plagues that devastated Egypt as prototypes for its own sequences of plagues (chs. 8, 9 and 16). The Exodus story is God's verdict on Egypt as well as Israel's deliverance. The twin aims of judgment and salvation are balanced finely.

Fundamentally God is in control from first to last, from Creation to Paradise, as Creator of the world and as architect of its ultimate salvation, even if present appearances seem to deny it. That our world, as God's creation, is important for John, can be demonstrated statistically: out of 250 occurrences of the word 'earth' (*gē*) in the New Testament, 82 are in Revelation. God's power is righteous, uncompromising against evil in all its forms. Therefore the religious community—those who are striving to serve God, and so are enduring more than an equal share of suffering and martyrdom at the hands of this world's evil powers—trusts that God's power will avenge them. The situation is depicted in dualistic terms (God and Evil), because Evil is a force to be reckoned with by God's servants. But, as John's consoling vision reveals, the evil forces are essentially self-destructive, at war among themselves. The human participants are still scared to witless panic or despairing cry; it is not obvious that the story will have a happy ending. But from the heavenly perspective, although God's power is locked in a death or life struggle, God's triumph is already being celebrated. And the New Jerusalem will assuredly descend to earth.

M. Eugene Boring (*Interpretation* 40/3, 1986, pp. 257, 260) analysed the theology of Revelation as a response to fundamental questions:

> Who, if anyone, rules in this world?
> What, if any, is the meaning of the tragic events which comprise our history?
> If there is a good God who is in control of things, why doesn't he do something about present evil?

The Apocalyptist's answer is: 'He *will*, for history is a unified story which is not over yet'. The reassurance is conveyed particularly in the hymns sung repeatedly in the worship of heaven. God has already acted. Christ is the Lord. God will go

on acting consistently. The Kingdom of God is not a matter of
uncertain speculation as to its coming. The coming of the
Kingdom was combined with the Christological confession of
Jesus' Lordship. God is Almighty (*pantocratōr*—see 1.8; 4.8;
11.17; 15.3; 16.7, 14; 19.6, 15; 21.22). The Church is invited to
join in the heavenly worship: 'Hallelujah! For the Lord our
God the Almighty reigns' (19.6).

As we saw in our reading through Revelation, John's
visionary experience began with a glorious celebration both of
the divine Creator and of God's world. But in the present this
gives way to a scenario of nightmare, a realization of the
extent of the crisis (as we might see it for example in ecological and environmental issues). As in the Roman Empire of
the first century, so again today there is a sense of how fragile
are the apparently self-sufficient social and economic systems.
The time of God's harvest is at hand, when he will call all
producers to account, and rescue the good produce from the
weeds. Harvest is a time of judgment; it is also a time for
triumphant celebration, as the God of Creation is enthroned
in glory and the reality of his ultimate power is fully acknowledged. For the Christian community which suffers in the
world—and cares desperately for the redemption of the
world—the fear and foreboding are held in tension with the
hope and joy expressed in the anticipatory hymns of heaven.
Here on earth there are still other powers with which the
church must reckon, powers that appear to rival God and seem
set to destroy, by means of their self-destructive impulses, not
only goodness but the whole creation.

4. *The Work of the Holy Spirit*

> The charismatic movement has made the doctrine of the Spirit
> into something rather cosy, but the elemental biblical imagery
> of wind and fire is anything but that. The Holy Spirit is the
> Comforter, but also the one who leads us from conventional
> thinking into all truth, the inspirer of the prophets and *the
> speaker, in St. John's vision, of blasting words to the churches.*

This quotation is from Tony Grist writing in *The Guardian*
September 10th, 1990, but the emphasis is mine.

'Let anyone who has an ear listen to what the Spirit is

saying to the churches.' This 'Hearing formula' is repeated in every one of the seven letters of chs. 2 and 3, and it is echoed at 13.9. The formula is thought to have originated with the early Christians; it is also found at Mk 4.9 and parallels, in the context of Synoptic gospel parables. J. Roloff (*Die Offenbarung des Johannes*, ZBK 18, Zürich 1984, p. 50) rightly sees the 'Hearing formula' as wider in application in Revelation than with the Synoptic parables. John's emphasis has moved away from esoteric ideas of grasping secrets (but see 13.18 for an intellectual variation). It becomes a prophetic warning and exhortation. The words are those of the Risen Lord speaking through inspired revelation. The Apocalypse has in this more localized way the sense of the continuity of the work of Jesus and the Holy Spirit that is established in the teaching on the Comforter in the Last Supper discourses of John's gospel (see 14.16-17).

It is important to recollect how open are the ideas in Revelation about missionary outreach. Potentially anyone who responds to the prophetic warning, and then repents, can be rescued. There is no predestined total of the elect, only a symbolic inclusiveness (144,000)—based on tribes of Israel— which then merges with the incalculable multitude (7.9). And so the Spirit's words to the churches are not only addressed to the elect; potentially the prophetic warning and exhortation can be heard by anyone. Anne-Marit Enroth says (*NTS* 36/4, 1990, p. 603),

> Characteristically the HF [Hearing Formula] is positive and open, for there is no connection with hardening and division of the hearers into two groups: those who do not hear and those who do.

The idea of hardening is prominent in the context of Mark 4 (see vv. 11-12; and compare Paul in Rom. 9.18; 11.7). This was a theological solution to the problem with which early Christians wrestled, as to why the gospel preaching was spurned. So it must be significant that, while the early Church context for this formula includes hardening, 'this conception is absolutely lacking from the Book of Revelation' (p. 603).

The nature of prophetic Christian preaching, and the call to repentance, is indicated by 14.6-7:

> Then I saw another angel flying in midheaven, with an eternal gospel to proclaim to those who live on the earth—to every nation and tribe and language and people. He said in a loud voice, 'Fear God and give him glory, for the hour of his judgement has come; and worship him who made heaven and earth, the sea and the springs of water'.

Revelation by angels corresponds in apocalyptic imagery to inspired prophetic utterance. This preaching is repeatedly designated by two terms ('the word of God'/'the testimony [of Jesus]') which are bracketed together (see 1.9; 6.9; 20.4). The essence of prophecy is in bearing testimony to Jesus (19.10; 22.9), who is himself the 'faithful witness' (1.5). We should not forget that the genitive in the phrase 'testimony of Jesus' can be both subjective and objective. This emphasis on divinely-inspired prophecy (not that Revelation itself should be called prophecy in distinction from apocalyptic—see above, Chapter 3) points to the significant role of prophets within the communities for which John wrote. Revelation helps us indirectly to understand the milieu of Christian prophecy.

Testimony/witness is a key idea in Revelation which leads actually (and etymologically) to martyrdom. The Greek words for it (*martus / marturia*) evolve in meaning in the context of this New Testament book. It becomes a complex idea, as Elisabeth A. Castelli describes it, 'of martyrdom as death and as witness (a telling) and as victory (an inversion of contemporary power relations, repression becoming exaltation)' (*Imitating Paul: A Discourse of Power*, Louisville 1991, p. 47). The visions of ch. 11 indicate how this witnessing is effective. Witness is an activity in the closest relation to Christ (Imitation of Christ) on the path from suffering to glory (see 1.5; 11.8). Revelation demonstrates a significant chain of witness from God, to Christ, to the angel, to the prophet, to the churches, to the world (see 1.1-2). God's reign is seen as universal in power, but it works towards its culmination through human agencies and representative individuals. Those who have the testimony are those who preserve Jesus' witness, declare it to the world, and suffer and die for it. What they declare is what Jesus himself reveals: the judgments and the sovereign authority of God.

Testimony/evidence is not simply what one has gained, like

a detective, and holds onto as the vital clue. It is something that needs to be communicated because, like the prophet of old, one cannot keep it to oneself. But the role of Christian witness evolves from the original job description in the act of presenting the message to the world. As Jean-Pierre Jossua OP writes in *The Condition of the Witness* (London 1985, p. 64),

> Something of what one wants to bear witness to emerges only in the act of witnessing...The word of God is only grasped in its meaning for today...by expressing itself and acting as a word of salvation, of pity, of hope for specific human beings, at a given time.

Conclusions

This chapter is short on firm conclusions, but has tried to explore the range of theological issues that need to be considered. We must look at the text in its own terms, as well as observing its relationships with other texts. But we must not seek to homogenize Revelation into a single statement of Christian doctrine and thereby conflate the meanings of originally independent texts. That is to do a disservice by ignoring the possibility of distinctive points of view.

It is still possible to evaluate the work in its own terms, yet regard it as but one component of the larger context of biblical theology, not only in the New Testament but in the perspective of the Old Testament as well. Because of the Apocalypse's multiple points of contact, it can emerge very positively from the panoramic consideration 'from Moses to Patmos'. The recent work of Brevard Childs (*Biblical Theology of the Old and New Testaments*, 1992) deserves close, but not uncritical attention. His assessment of Revelation is as follows (p. 321):

> The author has effected a profound alteration of the apocalyptic tradition on the basis of his understanding of christology. The whole apocalyptic scenario which he inherited has now been interpreted as completed action. It does not lie in the future, but in every apocalyptic cycle described, God now rules his universe and the kingdom has come (7.10; 11.15; 19.6). Satan has been defeated by the Lamb and cast out of heaven. The Anti-Christ has been conquered and salvation realized.

However, the writer of Revelation continues to use the apocalyptic vision to focus on the nature of the church's continuous struggle with evil, false prophets, and civil oppression. The biblical writer allows the eschatological tension between a heavenly and earthly reality to continue. Much like the Synoptics' use his attention turns to exhortation and a call for endurance even unto death (2.10).

Recommendations for Further Reading

Commentaries on the Book of Revelation:
It is hard to recommend more than a small number of commentaries in English; even these cannot be recommended unreservedly. Never rely on a single commentary! But a useful interaction can be obtained within a mixed group such as these four:

G.B. Caird, *The Revelation of St John the Divine*, Black's New Testament Commentaries, London: A. & C. Black 1966.

R.H. Charles, *A Critical and Exegetical Commentary on the Revelation of St John*, International Critical Commentary, 2 vols., Edinburgh: T. & T. Clark 1920.

Austin Farrer, *The Revelation of St John the Divine: A Commentary on the English Text*, Oxford: Oxford University Press 1964.

J.P.M. Sweet, *Revelation*, SCM Pelican Commentaries, London: SCM Press 1979.

Studies of the Book of Revelation:

Richard Bauckham, *The Theology of the Book of Revelation*, New Testament Theology Series, Cambridge: Cambridge University Press 1993 [the newest work on the list, treating the book's great theological importance but with admirable brevity].

A. Yarbro Collins, *Crisis and Catharsis: The Power of the Apocalypse*, Philadelphia: Westminster Press 1984 [essentially a sociological analysis of the book].

John M. Court, *Myth and History in the Book of Revelation*, Atlanta: John Knox Press/London: SPCK 1979 [authors should not recommend their own books, but this will serve to emphasize the interplay between inherited traditions and actual historical situations].

Colin J. Hemer, *The Letters to the Seven Churches of Asia in their Local Setting*, JSNT Supplements 11, Sheffield: JSOT Press 1986 [a splendid book combining first hand field work in Asia Minor with a survey of ancient sources and inscriptions].

E. Schüssler Fiorenza, *The Book of Revelation: Justice and Judgment*, Philadelphia: Fortress Press 1985 [a compilation from articles over an extended period, holding together issues of literary structure and historical-rhetorical situation].

Select Bibliographies

Chapter One—Revelation Revisited

Loveday Alexander (ed.), *Images of Empire*, Sheffield: JSOT Press 1991.
David E. Aune, 'The Form and the Function of Proclamations to the Seven Churches (Rev 2–3)', *NTS* 36.2 (April 1990), pp. 182-204.
John M. Court, *Myth and History in the Book of Revelation*, Atlanta John Knox Press/London: SPCK 1979.
Paul D. Hanson, *Visionaries and their Apocalypses*, Issues in Religion and Theology 2, Philadelphia: Fortress Press/London: SPCK 1983.
Anthony Kenny, *A Stylometric Study of the New Testament*, Oxford: Oxford University Press 1986.
Jürgen Moltmann, *God in Creation: An Ecological Doctrine of Creation*, The Gifford Lectures 1984–85, London: SCM Press 1985.
Daryl D. Schmidt, 'Semitisms and Septuagintalisms in the Book of Revelation', *NTS* 37.4 (October 1991), pp. 592-603.
Klaus Wengst, *The Pax Romana and the Peace of Jesus Christ*, London: SCM Press 1987.

Chapter Two—Reading Revelation by Themes

G.B. Caird, *The Revelation of St John the Divine*, Black's New Testament Commentaries, London: A. & C. Black 1966.
Austin Farrer, *The Revelation of St John the Divine: A Commentary on the English Text*, Oxford: Oxford University Press 1964.
C.H. Giblin, *The Book of Revelation: The Open Book of Prophecy*, Collegeville, MN: Michael Glazier, Liturgical Press 1991.
Sophie Laws, *In the Light of the Lamb—Imagery, Parody and Theology in the Apocalypse of John*, Good News Studies 31, Wilmington DE: Michael Glazier 1988.
John A.T. Robinson, 'Interpreting the Book of Revelation', in *Where Three Ways Meet*, London: SCM Press 1987, pp. 35-75.
J.P.M. Sweet, *Revelation*, SCM Pelican Commentaries, London: SCM Press 1979.

Chapter Three—Literary Character

David E. Aune, 'The Apocalypse of John and the Problem of Genre', *Semeia* 36 (1986), pp. 65-96.
James L. Bailey and Lyle D. Vander Broek, *Literary Forms in the New Testament*, London: SPCK 1992.

David L. Barr, 'The Apocalypse of John as Oral Enactment' *Interpretation* 40.3 (July 1986), pp. 243-56.

A. Yarbro Collins, 'Reading the Book of Revelation in the Twentieth Century', *Interpretation* 40.3 (July 1986), pp. 229-42.

John J. Collins (ed.), *Semeia 14—Apocalypse: The Morphology of a Genre* (1979).

Gabriel Josipovici, *The Book of God: A Response to the Bible*, New Haven: Yale University Press 1988.

Frank Kermode, *The Sense of an Ending: Studies in the Theory of Fiction*, New York: Oxford University Press 1967.

Klaus Koch, *The Rediscovery of Apocalyptic*, Studies in Biblical Theology 2.22, London: SCM Press 1972.

Gerard Mussies, 'The Greek of the Book of Revelation', in J. Lambrecht (ed.), *L'apocalypse johannique et l'apocalyptique dans le Nouveau Testament*, BETL 53, Leuven: Leuven University Press: 1980, pp. 167-77.

Gerard Mussies, *The Morphology of Koine Greek as Used in the Apocalypse of St John: A Study in Bilingualism*, Leiden: Brill 1971.

S.E. Porter, 'The Language of the Apocalypse in Recent Discussion', *NTS* 35 (1989), pp. 582-603.

E. Schüssler Fiorenza, *The Book of Revelation: Justice and Judgment*, Philadelphia: Fortress Press 1985 .

S. Thompson, *The Apocalypse and Semitic Syntax*, SNTS Monograph 52, Cambridge: Cambridge University Press 1985.

Chapter Four—Historical Setting

A.A. Bell, 'The Date of the Apocalypse. The Evidence of some Roman Historians Reconsidered' *NTS* 25 (1979), pp. 93-102.

A. Yarbro Collins, 'Dating the Apocalypse of John', *Biblical Research* 26 (1981), pp. 33-45.

A. Yarbro Collins, *Crisis and Catharsis: The Power of the Apocalypse*, Philadelphia: Westminster Press 1984.

Ian Hazlett (ed.), *Early Christianity: Origins and Evolution to AD 600*, (Essays in honour of W.H.C. Frend, London: SPCK 1991.

Colin J. Hemer, *The Letters to the Seven Churches of Asia in their Local Setting*, JSNT Supplements 11, Sheffield: JSOT Press 1986.

Martin Hengel, *The Johannine Question*, London: SCM Press 1989.

Brian W. Jones, *The Emperor Domitian*, London: Routledge 1992.

Robert B. Moberly, 'When was Revelation Conceived?', *Biblica* 73.3 (1992), pp. 376-93.

S.R.F. Price, *Rituals and Power: The Roman Imperial Cult in Asia Minor*, Cambridge: Cambridge University Press 1984.

John A.T. Robinson, *Redating the New Testament*, London: SCM Press, 1976.

Leonard L. Thompson, *The Book of Revelation: Apocalypse and Empire*, New York: Oxford University Press 1990.

Chapter Five—The Theology of Revelation

David E. Aune, *Prophecy in Early Christianity and the Ancient Mediterranean World*, Grand Rapids, MI: Eerdmans 1983.

Margaret Barker, *The Great Angel: A Study of Israel's Second God*, London: SPCK 1992.

Richard Bauckham, *The Theology of the Book of Revelation*, (New Testament Theology Series, Cambridge: Cambridge University Press 1993.

M. Eugene Boring, *Sayings of the Risen Jesus: Christian Prophecy in the Synoptic Tradition*, SNTS Monographs 46, Cambridge: Cambridge University Press 1982.

M. Eugene Boring, 'The Theology of Revelation', *Interpretation* 40.3 (July 1986), pp. 257-69.

Maurice Casey, *From Jewish Prophet to Gentile God: The Origins and Development of New Testament Christology*, Cambridge: James Clarke 1991.

Brevard S. Childs, *Biblical Theology of the Old and New Testaments*, London: SCM Press 1992.

John M. Court, 'Risen, Ascended, Glorified', *Kings Theological Review* VI.2 (Autumn 1983), pp. 39-42.

J.D.G. Dunn, *The Partings of the Ways*, London: SCM Press 1991.

Anne-Marit Enroth, 'The Hearing Formula in the Book of Revelation', *NTS* 36.4 (October 1990), pp. 598-608.

Paula Fredriksen, 'Apocalypse and Redemption in Early Christianity. From John of Patmos to Augustine of Hippo', *Vigiliae Christianae* 45.2 (June 1991), pp. 151-83.

Graeme Goldsworthy, *The Gospel in Revelation: Gospel and Apocalypse*, Exeter: Paternoster Press 1984.

Kenneth Grayston, *Dying, We Live: A New Enquiry into the Death of Christ in the New Testament*, London: Darton, Longman & Todd 1990.

Alan F. Segal, *Rebecca's Children: Judaism and Christianity in the Roman World*, Cambridge, MA: Harvard University Press 1986.

INDEXES

INDEX OF REFERENCES

OLD TESTAMENT

OTHER ANCIENT REFERENCES

INDEX OF AUTHORS